COLLINS GEM
ANTIQUE
MARKS

G000049031

COLLINS GEM
CRICKET

COLLINS GEM
DIETING

COLLINS GEM
DOGS

COLLINS GEM
FIRST AID

COLLINS GEM
INTERNET

COLLINS GEM
PREDICTING

COLLINS GEM
Ready
REFERENCE

COLLINS GEM
SHARKS

COLLINS GEM
WHALES
& DOLPHINS

COLLINS GEM
WHISKY

COLLINS GEM
WORD
PROCESSING

COLLINS GEM
Your PC

HarperCollinsPublishers

COLLINS GEM

ANTIQUE FURNITURE

Michael Pick

Consultant: Tim Sanders

HarperCollins*Publishers*

Michael Pick writes and lectures extensively on the decorative arts. He is Director of Stair & Company Ltd, specialists in English antique furniture, co-founders of The British Antique Dealers Association and The Grosvenor House Fair.

All pictures courtesy of Stair & Company except pages:
The Bridgeman Art Library: 14, 20, 73, 85, 92, 97(t), 104(t), 105(t), 152(mb), 202(t), 205(b), 235, 237; Christie's Images: 12, 18, 23, 63, 77, 82, 83, 96(t), 98(t), 104(m), 105(b), 106(t), 109(b), 119(b), 120(m), 121(b), 122(t), 134, 135, 146(t), 160(mt), 161(mt, b), 167(t), 186(t), 187(t), 196, 197(t), 202, 205(b), 219(t), 225; Phillips Fine Art Auctioneers: 13, 187(b), 204(t); Topham: 95, 106(b), 136(b); The Victoria and Albert Museum: 17, 24, 27, 81, 90, 104(b), 109(t), 121(t), 145(b), 186(b), 189(t), 191(t), 201(b), 202(t), 229.

HarperCollins Publishers
PO Box Glasgow, G4 0NB.

First published 1999

Reprint 10 9 8 7 6 5 4 3 2 1 0

ISBN 0 00 472344-9

Created and produced by Flame Tree Publishing, part of The Foundry Creative Media Co. Ltd
Crabtree Hall, Crabtree Lane, London SW6 6TY

Printed in Italy by Amadeus S.p.A.

 Contents

Introduction

AS with all forms of art appreciation, understanding the history, value and function of antique furniture is a complex matter: no two pieces of furniture are ever the same and nothing can ever be taken at face value. With this book you will be given the necessary information that will teach you how to use your own eyes to recognise styles, features and woods, helping to identify and date pieces of interest as well as explaining the developments and fluctuations in forms and characteristics throughout history. You cannot expect to become an expert overnight – most experts spend a lifetime absorbing knowledge and are continually amazed by new discoveries – but this book gives you the basic information about the historical background of evolving styles and craftsmanship and tells you how to recognise them. It also outlines the best places to buy antique furniture and how to care for it.

There is no substitute for continually looking at items and reading up on a chosen field of interest. This book will give you a general appreciation of the complexities involved and steer you towards an easy understanding of what you are looking at and why it was made. Hints on the more obvious pitfalls of copied or faked items are given, together with tips on aspects of furniture maintenance, as well as other useful information in special sections.

How To Use This Book

THIS compact book contains the basic essential information to the understanding and appreciation of British furniture. The book is divided into four parts, together with a Compendium at the end. The timeline on pages 10–11 gives an overview of the main periods in furniture-making and the major events and styles that characterised these eras.

Part One gives a chronological history of furniture design from the Middle Ages to the present day, detailing the progression and revival of certain styles and designs. Part Two, the central section of the book, gives a more detailed approach to identifying pieces of furniture by their various features; this is divided into feature sections, each one organised roughly chronologically within the shape of the feature for ease of identification, and detailing the typical date, background and notable characteristics of each feature. Beneath each feature are icons indicating the types of piece on which the feature can be found, a date and a cross-reference to more detailed information in the History of Furniture chapter. A key for this section is given opposite. Part Three offers information on how to buy and sell antique furniture and gives advice on the best places to view certain pieces. Part Four details the different types of wood used in furniture making and gives information on how to care for your antiques. The Compendium gives supplementary information, including a glossary of unusual or technical terms, the addresses of the main auction houses and associations, and a detailed index, which wil lead you to all the subjects covered in the book.

George III, English c. 1760–1790
Very simple elegance of a lightly decorated ring handle to a mahogany drawer front featuring a small keyhole cutout.

George III, English c. 1775–1810
Stamped back plate and integral drop ring emphasizing the circular motif of the inlays forming the contrasting timbers of a drawer front. Various designs and shapes based on this idea exist.

George III to Regency, English c. 1790–1830
Small, finely detailed, circular drawer pull with a circular stamped back plate. Various motifs exist in this style.

George III to William IV, English c. 1800–1830
Neoclassicism applied to a gilt ring handle with a lion mask motif, a version of many such handles were designed, but here it is purely decorative.

🏛 LEGS 🏛

THE PREOCCUPATION with Classical Antiquity runs as a theme through the centuries of leg design and reflects changing tastes and fashions when studied with the foot of a piece.

Egyptian, New Kingdom, 18th Dynasty c. 1550 BC
One of the earliest surviving chair legs in history from Tutankhamun's tomb. Characteristically its carved symbolic lions' heads, feet and inward support with gold leaf.

Regency, English, 1815
Ebonised, carved beechwood leg with gilt cross braces to leopard's mask pelt embellished leaf and paw foot. A direct reference to contemporary archaeology of discoveries. In the manner of George Smith.

Key / Icons

 Brackets

 Cabinets and wardrobes

 Chairs

 Chests and bureaux

 Mirrors

 Settees

 Stools

 Tables

 Torchères

 1760   Date reference

 p. 46   Page reference

A Illustration of the identifying feature

B Essential information about the feature, including notable characteristics

C Period and country of origin

D Icons indicating the different pieces of furniture on which the feature can be found

E Approximate date

F Cross-reference to the relevant period or style in the History of Furniture chapter

Periods and Styles Timeline

Period/Monarch	Date	Style Features
Ancient Egyptian	c. 3000–300 BC	Use of fine gilding, metals and ivory inlays
Roman Rule	c. 55 BC–440 AD	Introduction of sophisticated furniture to Britain
The Middle Ages	1066–1500	Coronation Chair made for Edward I, 1296, Gothic style
The Age of Oak (Tudor)	c. 1500–1650	Rediscovery of strong joints
Elizabeth I	1558–1603	English Renaissance
James I (Jacobean)	1603–25	Refined carving
Charles I	1625–49	Carolean style
Cromwell	1649–60	The Commonwealth
The Age of Walnut	c. 1660–1730	European influences on British designers
Charles II	1660–85	The Restoration; Franco-Italian styles
William & Mary	1689–1702	Arrival of Dutch craftsmen in England
Queen Anne	1702–14	Exotic timbers from the colonies

Period/Monarch	Date	Style Features
George I	1714–27	Early Georgian period
George II	1727–60	Middle Georgian period
The Age of Mahogany	c. 1730–80	Rococo and Gothic influences
The Age of Satinwood	c. 1760–1800	Marquetry and gilding
George III	1760–1811	Late Georgian period: exotic timbers from India and S America; Adam brothers
Prince Regent (Regency Style)	1811–20	Wars with Napoleonic France
as George IV	1820–30	Reintroduction of ancient Egyptian and Greek forms
William IV	1830–37	Revival of early 17th c forms
Victoria	1837–1901	Great Exhibition 1851; after 1870 Arts and Crafts movement
Edward VII	1901–10	Revival of Adam styles; Art Nouveau
George V	1910–35	First World War 1914–18; Bauhaus 1919–; *Paris Exposition des arts décoratifs*: Art Deco 1925; Art Moderne, 1930s
George VI	1937–52	Second World War 1939–45; Utility and Austerity
Elizabeth II	1952–	Festival of Britain 1951; plastics introduced

THE HISTORY OF FURNITURE
Introduction

FOR anyone seriously interested in collecting and appreciating furniture, a rudimentary knowledge of the development of furniture styles is essential. Pieces of furniture are usually first identified on the basis of the style visible from the outward appearance of the decorative parts and outline of, say, the legs.

But this is not the only necessary piece of information: design, quality of materials, craftsmanship and overall condition are equally important. Furthermore, in considering all these attributes together, you, the potential purchaser or viewer, must consider the aesthetic appeal of the piece of furniture, not least because its price tag will reflect someone else's opinion of all these

The throne of Egyptian pharaoh Tutankhamen, covered in gold leaf and iconographic carvings, c. 1330 BC.

attributes. You should ask yourself whether this coincides with your own opinion. Without an appreciation of all that is inherent in the particular piece of furniture you admire, you can neither form a valid aesthetic judgement nor be sure that you are spending your money wisely.

No two pieces of antique furniture are ever exactly the same to the trained professional eye. There are even variations between pairs of items or, say, sets of chairs. It is dangerous to believe that you can set an appropriate price merely by comparing an auction result with what you see in front of you. Second-hand cars lend themselves to this, as do many mass-produced objects, but not furniture. The more you know, the better armed you will be and the more pleasure you will gain from your furniture viewing. Remember, there are no limits to the extent of your knowledge, if you practise and train your eyes. First, however, you have to know what you are looking at, and so a basic outline of furniture history is imperative.

As you will rapidly discover, the styles and designs applied to furniture constantly reappear over the centuries, albeit in differing forms, and so part of the fun of looking at furniture is to identify how and why this happens. For example, a chair in the Egyptian taste favoured by rich fashionable English householders around 1820, has its roots in furniture favoured by the equivalent type of owner in the days of the New Kingdom during the 18th Dynasty, when Tutankhamen was pharaoh. If we consider that this was some time around 1330 BC, and that the means of constructing such a chair were no different from those employed by the British in 1500, then it is obvious that a study of furniture is also a study of human civilisation, with many fascinating areas in which you may choose to specialise.

The Middle Ages

Egyptian life influenced the ancient civilisations around the Mediterranean: Greek, Etruscan and Roman. The last introduced new furniture-making techniques to Britain, but these only lasted for the period of their occupation. Native skills slowly developed, reaching their zenith in the great cathedrals of the Middle Ages.

THE Romans brought their furniture-making skills with them to Britain, including the manufacture of bronze table-bases, but with their departure Britain sank into a long period of economic and social decline. The only remnant of Roman civilisation to remain in Britain's native furniture lies in the local techniques of chair making using plaited rushes,

End of a Roman funerary couch of carved bone, dating from the first century BC.

straw ropes or wickerwork. Few examples of these date from earlier than about 1830. All the craftsmanship involved in furniture-making disappeared: mortice and tenon joints, dovetails, veneering, inlays and metalworking were all known to the Romans, but were not revived in Britain until the Norman Conquest (1066) brought a new breed of conquerors, with their own architectural forms, to a semi-savage land.

EARLY DECORATIVE CARVING

WHEN YOU READ that no British furniture exists to be collected dating from before 1500, then the writer is referring to domestic pieces. The great ecclesiastical foundations of the Middle Ages were the instigators of enormous building projects; witness the many cathedrals built during this period. The skills of builder and carpenter were honed on such projects over several hundred years. If you wish to see superb early examples of wood carving and the way in which wood was used for such features as ceilings, fonts or pulpits, then there is a large number of examples to choose from. Always bear in mind that most cathedrals and churches have been altered over the centuries, and some were used as a source of wood in the nineteenth century for these making copies or fakes of early furniture. Much 'medieval' woodwork may therefore be of recent date and quite unlike anything actually produced in medieval times.

The skills taught and learnt through the construction of monasteries, abbeys and other ecclesiastic buildings over the period were slowly applied to settled domestic interiors as Britain became more orderly and thus prosperous. Until well into the 1500s, only the rich had domestic furniture that we would recognise as such.

The Age of Oak

The Age of Oak saw the beginning of domestic furniture design, at a time when even the rich owned few items of furniture. Such pieces were mostly portable and consisted of basic seating and storage. Advances in carpentry made panelling widespread during this period.

THE Age of Oak, as it is generally known to historians and collectors, was established by 1500 and lasted until around 1650. Even the rich had few pieces of furniture in their houses. They led itinerant lives, constantly attempting to consolidate or increase their power and possessions. Much useful furniture was therefore designed to be moved, hence the small chests, coffers and such items as 'X'-framed folding chairs, of which only museum specimens survive.

A SHOW OF WEALTH

A RICH MAN of the time would have had a house that reflected the monarch's palace in design and organisation. Visible signs of power were inherent in one large reception room, the hall, used for eating, receiving and public entertaining. Smaller living rooms and bedrooms were tucked away off this room. At one end of the hall the master's armchair, as symbolic as a throne, was set upon a raised dais in front of a solid table constructed of broad and long planks of wood, usually two, but sometimes three. Early examples rested on shaped solid trestles, but by 1500 a jointed structure was usual and the ends of the table-top were cleated. The lady of the house might have a smaller version of this chair, but generally used a stool, as did others of lesser rank around the table. Forms (benches) were used in the body of the hall for others lower down the social scale. In the private rooms, smaller chairs might be found, but stools were usual.

Other types of furniture slowly evolved. Benches had been built into the panelling of the walls by the fifteenth century and were also used as side tables or for storage, sleeping and as shelves. Later, movable benches with backs constructed like the room panelling were used as settles (an early type of settee). These were set in front of the large open fireplaces to shield people from draughts, and several might form a compartment within the hall. By 1500 they often had a hinged seat to give access to the storage space below. The development of carpentry into the craft of joining wood resulted not only in improved wall-panelling, doors or cupboard fronts, but also the extension of tech-niques to all furniture, so that armchairs typically had a panelled structure, even when their bases were left open by the 1580s.

Seventeenth-century carved and inlaid English oak armchair.

Early Methods of Furniture-making

Manufacturing techniques remained basic, with crude staple-hinged or wedged joints, until the rediscovery of the mortice and tenon joint.

THE basic techniques of furniture manufacture lasted for centuries, with joints crudely formed by simply hammering in nails and banding the result tightly with iron pieces. Iron was also used for staple-hinges on such items as dug-out chests formed from tree-trunks. Set against the remarkable finesse of the armour and chain-mail craftsmanship of the times, it is astonishing that furniture was so very basic and in ordinary houses seems to have

A Tudor side-cupboard combining ventilated food storage, showing Gothic tracery.

gone no further than such a chest or a three-legged stool. Yet as late as the fourteenth century, ordinary Londoners still squatted around a room to eat in unsavoury conditions. For the more sophisticated, trestle tables and benches or stools were constructed with wedged joints. Climatic changes such as dry summers and wet winters cause timbers to contract and expand, and such early joints were insecure. Insects, rough floors and treatment compounded the problem, explaining why few such pieces survive.

Carving was practised widely during the Age of Oak, with motifs changing from, for instance, Gothic to later linenfold patterns (these were two popular ones regularly revived), but first applied to panelled rooms and their furniture. 'Linenfold' refers to the regular undulating motif first seen on European furniture, derived from folded linen as stored in cupboards and coffers.

THE MORTICE AND TENON JOINT

THE REINTRODUCTION to Britain, by 1500, of the ancient Egyptians' superb discovery of the mortice and tenon joint truly revolutionised furniture construction. This method ensures that the mortice hole made in the upright leg or support of a piece was plugged by the tenon, or tongue, of the opposing member, such as a stretcher. Drilled through and plugged with a roughly shaped dowel or peg, such a joint was virtually immovable if the timber itself was tough enough to withstand use and adverse weather changes. Together with its widespread availability in central and southern Britain, this explains the popularity of oak, which is also rot- and termite-resistant, especially when oiled or stained. The use of oak ensured the longevity of many pieces of joined furniture, where the use of weaker timbers has largely resulted in their destruction.

The Development of Design

After 1500, economic advances, and those in carpentry and joinery, encouraged new items to be made, although chests were still used for many different purposes. In addition, pieces were often decoratively carved and then painted.

HOUSEHOLD FURNITURE

KING EDWARD I's Coronation Chair has all the attributes of a well-made and well-designed oak armchair of a European type that existed from 1000 for almost 800 years. The Gothic style of the back is typical of its date, 1296; it is rare to find

anything genuine from this period. However, by 1500 the combination of skilled joinery and the development of British society resulted in the smaller domestic rooms off a typical hall receiving more attention; chests, coffers, chairs, stools and beds were all usual. There were many smaller versions of chests and coffers in richer homes, for when important people travelled they often took many possessions with them, sometimes even their chairs and trestle tables.

King Edward I's Coronation Chair, with carved Gothic design, dated 1296.

NEW DECORATION

INNOVATIVE CRAFTSMEN must have been in short supply and not particularly well rewarded throughout this period, because furniture certainly evolved slowly in design, as did hand tools. The Egyptians of Tutankhamen's day used chisels, saws and – for smoothing wood – an adze, in addition to other tools for cutting and shaping inlays. Virtually identical tools remained in common use in Britain until the 1600s, thousands of years later. Typical pieces of furniture from this period include comparatively crude carved joined chests. Examples abound, but most are of dubious antiquity. Genuine ones were originally used for storage of everything, even serving as tables or beds when necessary. In the early 1500s pierced panels decorated side-cupboards and also ventilated them if they were used for storing food. Smaller hanging cupboards, such as hutches, began to evolve; usually these had turned spindles decorating the fronts. By decoratively turning timbers on a lathe for use in furniture construction and then painting the completed piece and its carvings, furniture took on a new and quite ornate appearance.

The folding 'X'-framed chair, also used in antiquity, was still used by the powerful, but non-folding versions with the frame close-covered by fabric similar to that of the cushions and back were now made as well. For centuries this chair provided the most comfortable form of seating, at a time when rich hangings and cushions on hard seats were not only a measure of economic status, but were also a source of necessary comfort. When we see early furniture today it is usually devoid of all such colourful decoration, and a leap of imagination is necessary to conjure up the far from drab scene it would have originally provided.

Elizabethan Furniture

The reign of Elizabeth I is best characterised by an ebullient, lavish decorative style. Pieces were generous to accommodate the wide, ornate clothes of the period.

F ROM 1500 to 1580 the shape of turnings and style of carvings became ever more exuberant. The English Renaissance occurred later than that of the rest of Europe and is marked by the adoption of neo-classical designs and motifs intermingled with free-flowing leaf motifs. Clothes were equally decorative. Look at a portrait of Queen Elizabeth I, *Gloriana*, and place her elaborate ruff and wide embroidered dress in the context of bulbous, carved, covered goblet-shaped legs or supports on tables or bedposts. The wide tables and armchairs had to accommodate such finery and merely formed the background to this display. Open or semi-enclosed side tables of three tiers, known as court cupboards, held an impressive display of silver as a tribute to the guests.

Carved details included references to the architectural details used in the houses of the time. By the end of Elizabeth's reign in 1603, carvings and details were particularly lavish on the fittings of houses. Marble was used for the Italianate fireplaces of the largest houses, which also had elaborately carved staircases and ceilings. Furniture details were copied from these decorative elements, including strapwork, fluted pilasters and even arcading on friezes and uprights. Chair backs at this date were often inlaid with leaf-like patterns of more unusual woods such as holly, heightened by bone inlays and

Elizabethan joint stool with inverted baluster-design legs, c. 1600.

enhanced with colour. The use of glass for windows, even in small houses, meant that interiors were now flooded with light. A fine example of this is Hardwick Hall in Derbyshire – the contemporary jingle 'Hardwick Hall, more glass than wall' is symbolic of the taste and progress of English civilisation by 1600. The mellow patina of wood furniture we love today would almost certainly have been hated by the Elizabethans!

THE PURSUIT OF COMFORT

THE MEASURE of comfort achieved is only understood by reading contemporary accounts: the skirts of the women and padded trousers of the men made sitting on hard surfaces endurable, but cushions were embroidered and stuffed full as a matter of course. Tangible evidence of comfort exists in the great four-poster beds of the period, into which the occupant could sink as though in a tent, although he would be lucky if not plagued by bed bugs. By 1600, with Queen Elizabeth's reign almost over, comfortable domesticity was feasible in smaller houses throughout the country, not just the large ones or those in cities.

James I and Charles I

B Y 1600, even modest homes benefited from convenient, light furniture. Charles I's accession in 1625 paralleled an interest in collecting paintings and textiles – visible possessions that demanded fine furniture to set them off. Practicality and beauty on a small scale were consciously sought after. Long dining tables were inconvenient in smaller houses, but drop-leaf tables on four legs could extend to double the length when needed. Another major innovation was the back-stool, a side chair (evolved from the usual joint stool) with a low back and seat, comfortably upholstered. Fixed, padded comfort was fashionable and upholstered settees were an important status symbol in great houses such as Knole in Kent.

Of course, earlier forms of furniture were not abandoned over-night; indeed, many joint stools were still being made in the 1800s, as were forms

Oak-framed and upholstered English chair, dating from the mid-seventeenth century.

of large oak armchairs. New lighter forms may have been fine in genteel urban or grander country settings, but for the majority of lesser rural or urban surroundings they were simply unsuitable.

A LIGHTER STYLE

IN THE PAST, stone or wooden floors were mainly used in the raised domestic quarters, and the hall usually had a clay floor strewn with many layers of rushes in various stages of unpleasant decay. This horribly insanitary habit lasted for centuries, to the consternation of visiting foreigners, until the more progressive years of the early sixteenth century. By 1560 floors were increasingly paved or boarded over, and it became usual to order furniture of a lighter construction. Although large oak armchairs were still used throughout Britain, more sophisticated lighter versions were made for the smarter, urban, monied classes.

COLLECTABLE FINERY

THE YEARS TO 1650 were not economically prosperous, and it is not surprising that British taste remained dominated by the truly antiquated obsession with sumptuous fabrics and hangings at the expense of furniture construction. King Charles I was particularly interested in French taste, because of his French-born queen, Henrietta Maria, but he amassed paintings and superb textiles for his new buildings, rather than exciting new forms of furniture, and his palace buildings were most notable for the ever-larger panes of glass in their windows. This high visibility of possessions encouraged the development of new forms of furniture.

Technical Developments

DOVETAILED joints meant the possibility of drawers on runners and drop-leaf tables – convenience married with elegant style. Technical developments continued, even during the Puritan Commonwealth, when over-elaborate forms of decorative detail were frowned upon and craftsmen concentrated on achieving simplicity with elegance and attention to finer construction. The preoccupation with expensive fabrics and trimmings was abandoned until the Restoration of 1660; as a symbol of indulgent lifestyles it was superseded by the honest craftsmanship of the joiner.

Although experiments with bobbin-turned, lighter structural forms occurred, by 1600 the main development resulted from the reintroduction of dovetailed joints into Britain. Applied to case furniture, this meant that fitted chests of drawers superseded the use of cumbersome top-lidded chests. Early drawers were suspended on runners fitting into grooves halfway down the side of the drawer, and the grain of the timber usually ran from back to front, a characteristic style until the 1680s and later in more remote areas. Smaller occasional tables were also made, and the large plank-topped dining tables were slowly replaced by versatile, iron-hinged,

drop-leaf tables. Greater versatility and elegance were demanded by a more sophisticated population, but always remember that the further a location was from London or flourishing centres of commerce such as Bristol, the more backward construction and design remained.

Communications were slow in general matters of taste, new forms were not always appreciated and were often inappropriate for less sophisticated surroundings.

THE COMMONWEALTH AND AFTER

NEVERTHELESS, DURING the years of Cromwell's Commonwealth, design developments occurred. Bobbin turnings on more lightly constructed chairs and tables became quite usual. Nor was oak the only timber used. In line with the Puritan creed, textiles and carvings were sober and restrained, but lighter woods were increasingly used, possibly as a form of passive resistance to the heavy dictatorship. Certainly by the time of the restoration of Charles II in 1660, easily carved walnut was increasingly favoured, with its lighter colourings and lively figurings. The use of brass-headed, tightly nailed leather upholstery is usually thought to be part of the strict Puritan code, but was in fact considered a very smart and comfortable style during the reign of Charles I and also became increasingly used after the Restoration of Charles II.

Walnut chair with turned stretchers and bobbin feet, dating from c. 1675.

The Restoration and After

The returning court of Charles II introduced
fashionable French styles and many foreign
craftsmen to Britain. They brought ideas such as
large, stuffed cushions and leg and foot details.

AN INFLUX OF NEW IDEAS

FURNITURE AFTER THE Restoration was heavily
influenced by the French taste experienced by the court in exile.
Just as wood-carvers and joiners of the Middle Ages drew on
Flemish and French examples and, later on, Franco-Italian
Renaissance influences to develop a British style, so furniture-
makers considered and adapted foreign influences in the late
seventeenth century and have done ever since. Technically,
the craftsman was becoming more adept; this was in part due
to the great numbers of foreign artisans who were now made
welcome in Britain and they brought their new skills and
designs with them.

After 1660, the lively spiral turnings used on walnut and
beech – both light strong woods – were also applied to other
timbers, such as oak, but were considered less fashionable.
Chairs, settees and stools were made with split-cane seats,
already popular on the Continent. Large stuffed squab cushions
completed the effect; the richer the owner, the more elaborate
the velvets, silks and trimmings. Needlework had always been
used, but at this time was not the most usual form of covering.
The stiffer large skirts, or farthingales (under-skirt hoops),
worn in the early 1600s by fashionable women had been
replaced by more clinging garments and, under Cromwell, by

simpler garb. The women of the Restoration wore flowing garments of less weight, needing less space on chairs or day-beds – now of elegant, slim construction.

DECORATED TABLES AND CHAIRS

DURING THIS TIME, the legs and feet of furniture also assumed a new decorative importance. The marriage of the king to the Portuguese Catherine of Braganza led to the under-scrolled toe being termed a 'Braganza' foot. The turnings of stretchers and legs had been supported on small bobbins or half-bobbins, a feature still found on some chairs and tables. The latter were now numerous in size and shape. Large drop-leaf tables with elaborate turned supports were usual. Smaller rectangular side- or centre-tables often had drawers in the frieze, and various types of small circular tables are still to be found, as are chests of drawers. These were sometimes veneered with thick pieces of unusual and decorative timbers on to geometric raised panels of the drawer front.

The Great Fire of London in 1666 resulted in a building and furnishing boom to replace lost items. The latest styles were much sought after and the in-fluence of this boom was felt throughout Britain.

Walnut table with outswept foliate 'Braganza' toes, named after Charles II's wife.

Cabinet-making

The end of the seventeenth century saw a taste for cabinets of elegant design, particularly lacquered examples from the Far East. Their superlative craftsmanship inspired many imitations. Gilding and ornate carving catered for increasingly sophisticated tastes.

Jardinière (c. 1815) showing the Oriental influences that became popular in the late 1600s.

THE ART OF THE CABINET

BY 1680 ANOTHER development in construction had taken
place that changed the nature of British furniture. Influenced
by Far Eastern examples, the cabinetmaker's craft now came to
the fore. Where previous generations of British men and
women had stored items in wall or hefty free-standing
cupboards, elegant finely jointed cabinets were now sought
after. Apart from continental examples, trade with the Far East,
especially Dutch and Portuguese links with China, resulted in
the import of glowing lacquered cabinets fitted with slim
drawers, all showing an artistic perfection unimagined at home.
Such cabinets were given a special place in the houses of the rich
by 1700. The simple shape of such cabinets is highlighted by
the increasingly intricate carvings of the silver-gilt bases and
shows the British response to a superior craft: it honed their
own artistic inspiration.

JAPANNING

LACQUERED FURNITURE was produced in Britain, often
without the elaborate effects achieved in China. The name
'japanning' was given to thinner and flatter home-grown
effects that naturally became more competent as time passed.
Similarly, and most importantly, the imitation of Chinese
techniques as an extension of the blue-and-white porcelain-
collecting craze, gave impetus to the refinement of cabinet-
making methods.

    Thinner drawer-linings and tiny joints were replicated on
walnut furniture within a remarkably short time. The use of
elaborate carving followed the influence of Daniel Marot's book
of architectural and interior designs with examples of the 'S'-
scroll legs united by high-arched and pierced, carved stretchers

and top-rails. Carved backs usually had a central pierced splat with a thin caned panel to either side and a caned seat supporting a thick squab. Later versions dispensed with caning and favoured the stuff-over upholstered seat and back.

RICH DECORATION

GILDING OF CHAIRS, side-tables and stands was an established continental taste favoured by the rich. The base wood is typically pine, on to which gesso is applied and gold-leaf placed, but oak and walnut were also given vestiges of gilding, the result known as parcel, or part-gilt. Carved torchères and mirror frames, in addition to various small boxes, all display the rapidly increasing sophistication in manufacturing skills and taste. A revolution occurred within the furnishing trade as demand soared, and is apparent from the application of so many crafts to the production of just one product, for example, an upholstered chair.

The advent of the sensational new 'S'-scroll leg, fashionably japanned; this shape derived from continental forms imported by foreign craftsmen.

William and Mary

Veneered furniture became popular under William
and Mary. Walnut, and to a lesser extent kingwood,
were the most desirable veneers, with others used
as inlays for cabinet furniture or table tops.

T HE accession of the Dutch ruler William of
Orange to the British throne, together with his
wife, Queen Mary, in 1689 provided the impetus for
the arrival of Dutch craftsmen into the British Isles.
They were particularly skilled in using both walnut veneers and
inlay and marquetry techniques. A new wave of prosperity
makes the late seventeenth century notable for the popularity of
veneered furniture. Oak or pine, often deal (yellow Norwegian
or whiter Baltic pine), were imported for the core construction.
Pine was particularly favoured because it was possible to achieve
a smooth surface and because glues adhere well to its porous
grain. New forms of writing bureaux, with drawers housed
beneath a sloping front, evolved into the bureau book-case with
a top section, often fitted with an elaborate arrangement of
drawers and pigeon-holes, beneath a cornice. The best are
veneered with walnut, although other veneers such as elm and
kingwood were used.

But walnut was, and is still, the most sought-after timber
used at the time, especially as a veneer on pine, a light timber:
even when full of clothes, a pine chest of drawers can be moved
easily. The demand became so great that quantities of walnut
were imported from Europe and, later, North America, for
veneering tops, sides and drawer fronts. Veneering became a

highly sophisticated art-form when used as marquetry, a surface resembling a jigsaw of elaborate flower-heads, foliage or monograms, achieved by using often coloured slivers or shaped slices of other rarer timbers, sometimes embellished by bone or metal inlays. Incised decoration depicting veins of leaves or flower-heads was enhanced by 'shading' the pieces in a heated sand-box before fitting them into the fretted-out pattern in the ground veneer and then dyeing with colour.

Veneers cut transversely from branches of laburnum trees were even more desirable if inlaid with circles of intersecting fine boxwood lines. Small drop handles and bun feet are usual, although later bracket feet may have been added to update the piece, or to replace worn-out originals.

A 'double domed' bureau bookcase, with turned walnut finials derived from Baroque sources, c. 1695.

Early Mirrors

New developments in glass manufacture resulted in
larger sheets and were popular with the rich eager
for mirrors. Often in carved frames, mirrors were
sometimes made as part of a matching set of
furniture or framed to complement bed-hangings;
the larger the mirror, the richer the client and the
more elaborate the frame.

THE development of glass making and the
creation of larger flat sheets was encouraged by a
demand for looking-glasses. Formerly, the
complicated process resulted in tiny sheets of mirror
for the very rich, usually surrounded by stump-work or
embroidered frames. Now larger, cushion-framed mirrors
reflected light and were made to match chests of drawers or
tables to form significant side-pieces. The best have elaborate,
fretted cornices, often incorporating ornate cyphers or initials –
symbolism was part of an educated person's display of learning.
These are now very scarce because of their fragile nature and a
later obsession with throwing away outdated types or decorative
parts of furniture.

The best mirrors have large sheets of rolled glass, produced
by established glass-houses in London and later in Bristol.
These were very expensive and are rare today, but many
attractive smaller versions can be found, some with candle
arms. The 'silvering' of mirror backs involved noxious mercury
processes and was highly skilled and dangerous to the health of
the workers.

The elaborate cornices of framed mirrors were echoed in scalloped and scrolled bedheads of carved wood. These were rarely gilded, but covered with fabric to match or replicate the hangings of a four-poster or fashionable half-tester bed, in turn matching the window curtains. Panelling of rooms was sometimes confined to the lower section of the wall, the dado, so that tapestries, or even stamped 'Spanish' leather panels, might be placed to greater effect.

RECREATIONAL PLEASURES

IN ADDITION to the craze for mirrors, whereby people could see themselves more clearly and so improve their appearance, collections of paintings were regularly found in houses of more modest means by 1700; the collection of Charles I, so despised by Cromwell, had set an unforgotten example and furnishings were undoubtedly selected to go with works of art in most houses, not just in those of noble families. Similarly, the taste for quite un-Puritan card-games was so widespread that new forms of gaming table were designed for the increasingly numerous affluent middle and upper classes, all influenced by fashions from the Continent, especially France.

Cushion-framed mirror with a kingwood frame, embellished with panels of floral marquetry derived from Dutch examples, c. 1690.

The Age of Walnut

WALNUT was the fashionable timber for some 70 years (*c.* 1660–1730) throughout this period. European influences, and those from farther afield, continued to inspire British design from 1660 and the Restoration of Charles II to the reign of George II. The reign of William and Mary (1689–94) merely cemented the influence of foreign craftsmen and the use of modified foreign styles.

FOREIGN INFLUENCES MODIFIED

BY 1700 The Age of Walnut was well established and new shapes were successively fashionable. By 1690, a slim, turned baluster leg with turned toe was used on both seating and tables, as well as cabinet stands. Usually united by flat, scrolling stretchers, often with a central finial turning, more important gilded pieces had square, tapering legs and resembled earlier Franco-Italian Renaissance architectural details. The influence of Italian designers on the rest of Europe had also affected British architects and designers, most famously Inigo Jones (1573–1652), then later, at the height of the Age of Walnut, Christopher Wren (1632–1723) and many subsequent British architects. Certainly the cabriole leg (see p. 40) evolved from Italian and Chinese designs with French and Dutch influences.

NATIVE PRODUCTS

WALNUT WAS USED for all types of furniture in the solid or as veneers; cabinet pieces of great quality have quarter-veneers, with herring-bone inlays to the tops, drawer fronts and even sides of the finest small chests of drawers, dressing tables or 'low boys'. Together with wider but shallow low chests of drawers with fold-over tops known as 'Bachelor's Chests', these remain the most desirable pieces, especially if they have superb colour, figure and a glowing patina. Technical innovations of the era include the design of the folding card table, the best examples resembling a small side-table with a hinged top opening to reveal a covered surface with candle stands and money scoops. The best have concertina frames, extending the friezes in a folding hinged action so that a leg is then at each corner. The gate-leg action previously used became the province of the less-skilled craftsmen or the choice of a less sophisticated client. Because of the building boom of the early 1700s in the larger cities, great quantities of furniture were made and so every purchaser had to consider carefully and order accordingly.

Small kingwood veneered secretaire cabinet with marquetry door fronts.

The Cabriole Leg

THE cabriole leg proved to be one of the most technically exciting developments in the history of furniture, and by 1710 fashionable clients had seized upon the form and saw it applied in walnut to new, simpler forms of furniture. It depends on a central downward point of stress coinciding with the centre of knee and foot.

The most elegant designs in walnut dispense with stretchers and rely on the beauty of a simple leg on an unadorned pad foot. Chairs have hoop-shaped backs with a flat vase-shaped central splat and a balloon-shaped drop-in seat, the best with a veneered frieze and back. Arms were of the curved 'shepherd's crook' type, but soon became outswept on short, scrolled supports. This form was found on upholstered settees and wing chairs; stuff-over wing chairs often had exaggerated scrolls to the ears.

THE INFLUENCE OF KENT

BY THE 1720s the knees of chair legs were often carved with a shell motif, also used on friezes and the interiors of bureaus and on many gilt-gesso mirror frames and side-tables. The tops were given a characteristic punched ground and strapwork decoration, echoing Elizabethan patterns of plaster ceilings from the previous century. The best of such gilt- or white-decorated pieces were designed by William Kent, or inspired by his magnificent examples. These drew on Venetian designs and were always used for the greatest decorative schemes of the time such as those at Houghton, Norfolk. Yet the motifs used on larger side-tables, such as the hairy paw feet, and pediments on mirrors, were scaled down by others for use in smaller rooms of less illustrious owners.

In the early 1900s, Kent's designs were often copied for the houses of the rich and, along with all walnut furniture in the styles of the early 1700s, must be inspected with extra care.

Walnut furniture was not only copied in the 1870s, but also heavily faked for the strong American market that was already seeking English antiques. Much of the early eighteenth-century veneered walnut furniture used imported Virginian timber and there were flourishing American East Coast cabinet-makers at that time. However, American furniture styles have distinct peculiarities and so confusion is rare between the two. Most native good antique early American furniture is vastly more expensive than its British counterparts.

Japanned, tri-form cabriole leg terminating in a pointed toe. An English refinement of Continental examples, c. 1710.

The Age of Mahogany

Lacquer remained popular, but was overtaken by
the craze for mahogany – a beautifully figured,
dense, carvable wood – between around 1730 and
1780. Rococo influences, and revived Gothic ones,
were utilised in designs.

THE taste for lacquered or japanned furniture
was constant throughout the first decades of the
1700s, from the reign of Queen Anne through to that
of George II. Lacquer represents a highly difficult
area even for the specialist, as connoisseurs were collecting it by
the 1870s. A steady stream of faked or, at best, copied, bureau
bookcases has been produced for well over 100 years – at one
time simple oak pieces were adapted, partly accounting for the
paucity of such pieces on the market. Genuine pieces of scarlet
lacquer, made by the great cabinet-maker Giles Grendey and sold
in quantity abroad, rarely appear on the market and command
enormous sums. The same applies to chairs, card tables, clock
cases, and chests decorated with green, black and particularly rare
white lacquer; examples of bureau bookcases in white lacquer are
among the greatest triumphs of British furniture-making and
many lacquered pieces were made for export.

A TASTE FOR MAHOGANY

BY 1730 the extraordinary building boom of the time had
subsided, but it was followed by an insatiable demand for
imported mahogany. Although duties on this wood were
not abolished until 1721, it had been used for some time,

Japanned and lacquered drawer fronts in the 'Chinoiserie' manner, inspired by authentic Far Eastern examples of lacquer or porcelain.

Dished-top, small centre table with mahogany tripod base, c. 1765.

certainly during the Restoration, as it came from British colonies and could advantageously be re-exported to the Continent. A devastating frost had killed off most of Europe's walnut trees, leaving a large stock of walnut timber for future use, but apart from this wood, mahogany was the preferred material because of its dense grain, giving a steel-like quality that lends itself to crisp carving; it is also resistant to termites and rot and can be given a beautiful finish. Early on, this was often obscured by the fact that it was stained a bright red colour, luckily a short-lived fashion as The Age of Mahogany blossomed, but nevertheless a treatment often preferred by customers.

ROCOCO AND GOTHIC INFLUENCES

FURNITURE STYLES overlapped; the later development of the cabriole leg style – with acanthus carving to the knees and a claw-and-ball foot – was derived from Ancient Roman designs and was made first in walnut and then in mahogany. There was a taste for the French rococo developing in sophisticated London circles, and by the 1740s Matthias Lock had success with published designs depicting a remarkably varied range, including tortuous carved frames and pieces boasting mythical birds amongst rocks and foliage. As an extension of the taste for the bizarre, Gothic designs were reinterpreted, notably by Batty Langley in 1742. They found their most famous supporter in Horace Walpole, who deployed the style in his house, Strawberry Hill, Twickenham. Walpole was one of the first poeple to collect early British furniture, and the reinvented Gothic details were termed 'Gothick' to distinguish the fanciful new style from the old.

Thomas Chippendale

THOMAS Chippendale (1718–79), the most famous name in the history of British furniture, revolutionised the art of chair and cabinet design. All his own rare pieces share the sheer technical mastery of his craft, and a plethora of designs were created to satisfy a huge demand. Many of these were based on his designs, but there were other books and many cabinet-makers.

FORMATIVE INFLUENCES

ROCOCO AND NEO-GOTHIC ('Gothick') styles coexisted from the 1740s, commissioned by affluent people in search of novelty. However, the two styles were also fused by designers. London designers led the way, with Vile and Cobb producing pieces for the court and reflecting a more sober late-Baroque style with serpentine shapes and heavy carving. Their important work was studied by Thomas Chippendale, who not only produced chairs with rococo 'French' cabriole legs and 'Gothick' open-carved backsplats, but also made his designs famous by publishing his own book of furniture designs, the justly famous *Gentleman and Cabinetmaker's Directory* of 1754. Although there were other pattern books, this was the first to be devoted exclusively to furniture and had an enormous influence, bringing its author commissions from some of the most powerful families in the country.

THE CHAIR DEVELOPS

CHIPPENDALE SUCCEEDED in harnessing the lightness of the best walnut furniture to the much denser and sombre-

Mahogany drawing table with cabriole legs; a design popularised by Thomas Chippendale, c. 1765.

looking mahogany. His carvers achieved miraculous feats of delicate tracery, particularly on the open backs of dining chairs. Where once there had been numbers of chairs set against the wall and brought out for groups to eat around circular tables, there were now sets of a larger number of chairs, usually free-standing, with the ritually important armchairs still made for the master and mistress of the house. Original armchairs from the eighteenth century are always up to two inches wider than side chairs and were intended to impress. Many such sets were also made for drawing rooms and include a chair-back settee en suite, although day-beds only survive in rare cases.

Although Chippendale is associated with the classic claw-and-ball foot on a carved cabriole leg, he designed and made a wide range of furniture in his workshops. Dining chairs with upholstered seats and backs, on square chamfered legs united by pierced stretchers, or on cabriole legs with scroll toes, were quite usual by 1765. He also catered for the Chinoiserie craze, with designs for pierced fret legs on tables and chairs, these also having latticed sides and backs. Even beds resembled small pagodas. His designs were usually fused with carved Gothic motifs and are a very British view of the Orient. Refined tools, including the plane and the use of wood screws, enabled the creation of remarkable effects.

Wall brackets with rocaille (shell or rock) decoration popularly associated with Thomas Chippendale's designs, c. 1760.

Rococo

THE extreme continental style of rococo brought sinuous curves to many items of furniture. Watered down by sober British tastes, it was superseded by a resurgence of neoclassical carving on all kinds of pieces.

NEW SHAPES

ELABORATE EFFECTS were familiar from the continental craze for rococo. This came later to Britain but, even though watered down, made play with sinuous curves. The popular serpentine outline of furniture, already familiar from Baroque examples, is difficult to achieve, but was applied to large side-tables, ornamental serpentine-shaped chests of drawers known as commodes, and even chairs. All are represented by the particular triumph of Chippendale's designs and the skills of the craftsmen. Similarly, upholstered camel-backed settees of the mid-eighteenth century have great scrolled arms and are wide and deep, demanding large cushions. Low library chairs are also wide, but generally have thinly padded upholstered backs, for the wider span of fabrics now used in upholstery demanded extra skills as prized as those of the cabinet-makers.

The elaborate furniture of the mid-eighteenth century was matched by extravagant clothes. These were wide and spreading, using much fabric in the frock-coats of the men and wide sweeping skirts of the women. The broad, airy nature of the best mid-eighteenth century furniture reflects this, and the large-paned windows and generous size of fireplaces, now fuelled by coal, highlight Britain's rapid industrialisation and economic success.

Skills were constantly refined and new ideas formed the stuff of success. Bureau bookcases of the 1750s no longer had the earlier mirrored or panelled exteriors, but instead boasted glazed doors with thin astragal mouldings, miracles of lightness above the fitted interiors and the drawers below. Carving was usually neo-classical in inspiration. To match the plasterwork of a room, such pieces have carved dentil cornices above the top friezes, the best with swans-necks frequently embellished with

*Mahogany framed
side chair with
rococo 'c' scrolls and
shell and
leaf motifs.*

fretted carving, usually pierced in a manner that is more Oriental than neoclassical. Carving was applied to legs, canted corners, feet and the edges of tops.

BEWARE IMITATIONS

BY 1890, HOWEVER, such furniture was already collected and many plain items, such as tripod tables, were given carving, or were completely faked from components of other pieces. For instance, very few examples of early clothes presses (wardrobes) have survived, whereas all houses seem to have possessed glazed bookcases! Again, it can be difficult to detect such deceit unless you have seen many examples and are familiar with the correct balance of an original design. Of course, the grandest houses had large rooms, but there is an airy expansiveness about all the best furniture of the period that is in tune with the stylised, idyllic neo-Palladian lifestyle attempted in the great houses.

Carved giltwood chair with rococo foliate patterns, c. 1740.

Mahogany tripod table, embellished with neoclassical carving, dating from c. 1765.

The Grand Tour

THROUGHOUT the eighteenth century it was usual for young men of means to make a Grand Tour through Italy as part of their education. Often with a tutor, they would sketch the sights: the richer brought paintings and sculpture back to Britain, where they commissioned houses in which to display their treasures.

ROBERT ADAM

THE INFLUENCE of the Grand Tour upon the taste of the century was profound. Travellers' sketches were often referred to when ordering new rooms or complete houses. The architect-designer Robert Adam, for example, made and published his drawings of Antique Roman remains, even describing any remaining colour schemes, and after 1760 he was the most sought after architect-designer. The replication of such influences in the fashionable rooms of the time is most inventive in the design of furniture and can be seen in such houses as Osterley Park in Middlesex, or Kedleston in Derbyshire. Although many ancient types of furniture were discovered carved on marble or stone or painted on walls unearthed during archaeological excavations, few were practical for British life in the second half of the eighteenth century. When Adam could persuade a client to adopt them, as in the Etruscan Room at Osterley Park, the results were dazzling.

Ancient Roman architectural motifs, however, were increasingly adapted for furniture. By 1770 the fluted, tapering, turned leg was used on chairs, tables and cabinets, and more obviously on carved bedposts. Favourite devices include the stylised anthemion (honeysuckle) flower, carved paterae, recurrent forms of the acanthus leaf and the use of inlays, combining all together with trailing wheat husks or ribbons. Mahogany remained the most usual ground timber, but it was cross-banded with other lighter woods including tulip- or satinwood.

Delicately modelled carved gilt gesso and off-white decorated shield-back chair, typical of the Adam period. The shape accommodated the elaborately skirted clothes of men and women, c. 1785.

THE PALLADIAN INFLUENCE

ANDREA PALLADIO (1508–80), the Italian Renaissance architect of Antique Roman-style villas near Vicenza in the region of Venice, influenced generations of British designers and architects from Inigo Jones in the first half of the seventeenth century to the Adam brothers in the late eighteenth century. His book of designs is still studied today and his completed buildings have always attracted many admiring visitors.

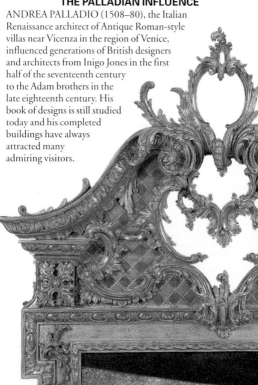

THE PEMBROKE TABLE

THE USEFUL PEMBROKE table, a small drop-leaf occasional centre table on small casters, began as a 1750s' sturdy square-legged design with a solid top, and legs joined halfway down by a wide shelf, enclosed by brass chicken wire with doors to one end. Food could thus be safely kept out of harm's way, an updated mobile version of the immobile sixteenth-century hutch. By 1780, the evolution of ever-lighter construction led to such tables being given serpentine-shaped leaves and then fashionably oval ones, on slim tapering legs, and with decorative tops often having inlaid panels of rarer, more exotic woods.

Neo-Palladian influence visible in the outline of this carved gilt and gesso frame overlaid with intricate rocaille decoration, a peculiarly British style of supreme elegance.

The Age of Satinwood

Satinwood was used for fine veneers, and its use
coincided with a revival of intricate marquetry in
free-flowing designs. Gilding and ormolu were used
to create a dazzling display of wealth.

 T HE Age of Satinwood arrived with the import
of this exotic, dense tough wood. It was used for
fine-cut veneers, and only rarely for components
such as chair legs, even for the very rich. The thick-
cut veneers of the late 1680s had long been supplanted by
thinner ones achieved by refined saws, a product of Britain's
technological achievements during the first Industrial
Revolution. By the 1800s there were larger furniture
workshops, with some mechanised machinery and a system of
component manufacture.

THE MARQUETRY REVIVAL

AS IN ALL periods marked by enormous economic progress,
there was a taste for reviving and refining older styles. A revival
of the marquetry skills so prized by the subjects of William and
Mary is evident in the number of inlaid tops – it also adorns
side and card tables and covers elaborate commodes (some of
the grandest of these were made for show and had no other use).
The inlays and marquetry of the late eighteenth century are
finer and less rigidly floral than those of the late seventeenth
century. A variety of bandings and motifs were used, such as
neoclassical vases, formerly unthought of. There was a passion
for the study of the classics, and mythological references were

often included in the decoration of furniture as well as rooms. A study of original examples will rapidly acquaint you with the differences between earlier and later styles and teach an appreciation of the more advanced techniques employed.

GILDING AND ORMOLU

THE ART OF THE gilder had been honed to a similar peak. Adam's designs for mirrors involve equally delicate tracery and skilled carving to achieve filigree effects that are usually intended to complement the designs of pier tables or commodes beneath. Throughout the eighteenth and nineteenth centuries, gilding was used as an ostentatious show of money and power. Thus, gilded furniture was very bright in appearance and regilding was usual. The toned, distressed effects we admire today are a product of twentieth-century taste. Combined with bright colours in a room, the original effect was intended to dazzle. This was continued in the refinement of ormolu mounts typically applied to the very best furniture from the days of Vile and Cobb, first as elaborately contrived handles, but then as feet or corner mounts. These were used sparingly except on the best pieces and copied French examples. The best craftsmanship remained French until Matthew Boulton began to manufacture fine mounts at his Soho works near Birmingham.

Mahogany sideboard with ormolu handles, c. 1790.

Hepplewhite and Sheraton

> Furniture for the middle classes was well-proportioned, made of good wood with fine details. Hepplewhite absorbed Adam's and Chippendale's work to produce graceful new designs, while Sheraton added novelty to fine craftsmanship.

QUIET BEAUTY

WHILE THE RICH often had gilt, the expanding middle classes bought more sober, straightforward and useful furniture, such as the mahogany sideboard, a side-table often with a serpentine or bowed shape and a kneehole effect produced by the use of deep drawers, one at each end supported by short legs. With pieces such as this, veneers were carefully selected and applied to show flame or fiddle-back figuring, heightened by beautifully proportioned handles with embossed back-plates. New dining tables were designed and made with solid

mahogany leaves on turned supports with outswept feet, showing the same interest in the timber sections. The Lancaster firm of Gillow produced quantities of such furniture, exporting their products worldwide, often as an early form of 'flat-pack' to the British in India or to America, only beginning to industrialise.

Carved and turned mahogany chair with neoclassical details popularised by Adam, including acanthus leaf and fluted legs.

HEPPLEWHITE

THE POSTHUMOUSLY published designs of George Hepplewhite epitomise an established taste for a light style, sometimes embracing French Louis XVI influences, with curves and at other times straight, almost plain lines with square tapered legs on thin toes. Shield or oval backs, made popular by Adam and widely used by all designers and makers, were ever lighter in construction and carving, thin upright splats, for example, forming Prince of Wales carved feathers in the back. The shape of the back characteristically floats on the two side supports; until the later 1760s, backsplats were joined to the middle of the seat back. Hepplewhite's *Cabinet-Maker and Upholsterer's Guide* (1788) sums up the accepted taste of the time, largely formed by Adam and his patronage of the workshops of such craftsmen as Chippendale and William and John Linnell, three outstandingly gifted craftsmen whose lives and work are well documented and will repay study.

SHERATON'S DRAWING BOOK

THOMAS SHERATON, the last (but not least) of the famous names of the late-eighteenth century, was the author of the widely used *Drawing Book*, published in 1793. This is striking for the number of metamorphic designs included. Tables become steps, drawers open to reveal fitted easels and Sheraton expanded the already familiar practice of fitting the top drawers of chests of drawers with brushing or writing slides, beneath which are all manner of compartments and boxes. Novelty and high craftsmanship were accepted as usual, as the style changed to neo-Grecian designs of chairs or tables influenced by the work of Henry Holland, famous for his work on the lavish rooms commissioned by the Prince Regent.

Regency Style

THE Regency style is named after the Prince Regent, son of George III, who was head of state in place of his ill father. He famously created lavish decorative schemes at Carlton House, Windsor Castle, Buckingham Palace and the exotic Brighton Pavilion. The beginning of the nineteenth century was marked by the Napoleonic Wars and instability at home, so the full Regency style came slowly to be represented by a simple neoclassicism.

A COMFORTABLE STYLE

BY 1800 THE SEATS and backs of chairs were lower, the latter typically with 'X'-shaped splats beneath broad curved toprails. Cabinets or tables were still often painted with mythological figures or floral or foliate panels, but the scale of the furniture was smaller; typically, dining chairs were lower and on turned legs with thicker, squared stuff-over seats. This was not simply the taste of the middle class; many grander houses were redecorated in this more congenial style. Bergère armchairs reflect this search for a new elegant comfort and are made for the slim-fitting clothes of the period.

Regency chair showing Antique Roman foliate designs.

Ebonised 'X' frame open armchair of the Regency period.

NEW WOODS

WRITING TABLES and desks became slimmer in outline and, for example, the compact Pembroke table was superseded by the wide rectangular sofa table with short, hinged flaps and two drawers in the shallow frieze. The taste for new and exotic timbers is witnessed by imported rosewood or kingwood.

These timbers are distinguished by their pronounced markings and deep colours when new. They were used as veneers on the finer pieces – for example on the many smaller work-tables fitted with fabric bags beneath – and most have now faded to paler shades.

Nests of small tables and slim side cabinets (chiffonniers) were similarly veneered, although mahogany remained the usual wood, especially for more formal dining furniture such as extending tables or sideboards. The popularity of smaller breakfast tables, with central columns on four splayed feet and using vividly figured veneers and bandings, started a new fashion. Originals of these useful smaller pieces are now difficult to find and expensive.

EXOTIC SPLENDOUR

THE MIDDLE PERIOD of the Regency style, around 1815, is marked by the introduction of new forms of furniture drawn from Antique sources, mainly those of Egypt and Greece, although Roman and Indian influences are also found. There was also a continuing fascination with the Far East. The Brighton Pavilion was an atypical form of exotic decoration, with diverse influences combined to produce such items as chandeliers with dragons and a Chinoiserie bedroom for the Prince himself. Apart from plumbing, new features abounded in this building. The bamboo stair-rail was in fact made of cast iron and the chandeliers were lit by gas, significant indications of the rapid progress made in Britain, where ancient decorative forms and styles were used to recreate the world of the past without its disadvantages.

Painted and gilt beechwood neoclassical chair from the Regency period.

French Influences

> The Prince Regent took the lead in collecting recent
> and old French furniture dispersed as a result of the
> French Revolution in 1789, so Boulle-work (shaped
> brass inlay) became fashionable again. Britain at
> war continued to absorb foreign craftsmen; emigrés
> and foreign influences blended into a
> patriotic style of its own.

CELEBRATING VICTORY

BRITISH WARS with Napoleonic France between 1805 and
1815 led to distinct influences on furniture design. The
Egyptian motifs made fashionable by French archaeological
discoveries were given impetus by battles there. Examples of
this craze include cabinets with crocodile mounts and a day-
bed like a stylised scaly model on reptilian legs. The military
influenced sabre leg, a form of those found on ancient Greek
klismos chairs, was a popular reminder of Wellington's land
victories, and when combined with the rope-twist top-rail or
horizontal backsplat, also formed a patriotic reminder of
Nelson's victories at sea. Such chairs were typically made of
mahogany, but the passion for light, strong beechwood
persisted from the late 1790s and so many dining chairs were
decorated black and gilt and had caned seats with squab
cushions, a reversion to the practical style of the late 1600s.
Sometimes the backs of dining chairs had caned panels
inserted for greater lightness and comfort. Drop-in seats were
also used for more formal dining chairs and as the 1820s
progressed, rosewood was also used.

Nelson's victorious naval battles and Wellington's successes in the Napoleonic Wars influenced fashionable decoration as demonstrated by the inclusion of rope motifs, stars and musket balls.

BOULLE-WORK

BOULLE-WORK WAS a replication of the brass inlay invented by the French designer André Charles Boulle (1642–1732), whose designs and idea of the inlay were a metal version of marquetry. This was then applied to table-tops, usually as a broad band around the edge of, for example, a circular table-top. The very rich had extremely elaborate writing tables and cabinets veneered with rosewood or ebony and inlaid with a variety of Boulle-work. Most people were content with a variety of ormolu mounts applied to chairs, cabinets and tables and traces of brass inlay, already used in the 1740s by German craftsmen working in London. They were using skills popular in cities such as Augsburg, but never very much used in Britain until the Regency period. Even then the finest metal mounts were French, in spite of Britain's metal technology and the earlier work of Matthew Boulton.

A HAZARD FOR THE COLLECTOR

BOULLE-WORK and metal inlays are a hazard as the shrinking or expansion of the ground timbers plays havoc with the components of the design. Never attempt to replace pieces

yourself, but seek competent advice, as the bad repair of such inlays will ruin the piece and its value. Bad repairs often prove insuperable because too much has either been altered or disfigured for ever.

Ormolu mounts on a mahogany chair, a symbol of luxury, c. 1810.

The Spread of Fashion

ANCIENT Egyptian and Antique-inspired styles continued to be popular, and the rich continued to aspire to fashions adopted by the highest in the land. Better communications and the printing of designs in journals spread fashions, and cheap imitations flourished.

TAMING EXOTIC INFLUENCES

IN ADDITION TO the Prince Regent, two furniture enthusiasts of the time had enormous influence. Thomas Hope was a rich amateur and designed for himself, publishing

the famous *Household Furniture and Decoration* in 1807. He influenced other designers by illustrating many of his own interiors and pieces of furniture, taking ideas directly from the French designer Percier and moulding Egyptian and Classical motifs into a domesticated vision of the Antique. Chairs with lions' heads at the ends of arms, and the front or even back legs as those of the animal, complete with paws,

Lion's paw foot, inspired by ancient Egyptian styles.

were an extension of the ideas practised in the eighteenth century, but given true archaeological form, being based on a study of examples depicted on pots. Tables with star motifs, cabinets with geometric bone and ebony inlays in the mahogany, and new forms of writing table with shaped slab supports were usual. Hope also influenced the author of another pattern book, the cabinet-maker George Smith.

The Graeco-Roman couch emerged as an elegant day-bed, with scrolling ends and on short sabre legs, already popular in France in the 1790s but with small turned feet, a style also used in Britain and similarly applied to sofas (as settees were called after Ottoman influences). Such feet are also found on cabinets and chiffoniers as well as chairs, where casters were favoured on the larger caned bergère variety. Upholstery tended to be tight, but as elaborate as the draped curtain effects made popular by the many illustrated journals such as *Ackermann's Repository*.

THE SPREAD OF IDEAS AND IMITATIONS

JUST AS FASHIONS in clothes were disseminated by the range of papers devoted to social news and developments, so furniture styles were more rapidly spread around the country. In the second half of the eighteenth century, furniture was easily transported on the growing canal network; the grandest styles were often made in lesser woods and were decorated, not necessarily just for the rich. The use of beech in furniture-making was widespread, but the decorative painted effects are so easily replicated and are so all-concealing that it is necessary to have not simply a good eye for the original, but also to be thoroughly convinced of the antiquity of a piece before parting with any money.

New British Style

In the first half of the nineteenth century, a revival of
'Gothick' was superseded by renewed interest in
true Gothic, sparked by a fascination with the
Middle Ages, part of the proliferation of influences
from abroad.

A RETURN TO GOTHIC

WHILE BRITAIN WAS influenced by so many foreign styles,
there was also a distinct trend towards former English styles,
and a lingering romantic vision of what Britain had been before
industrialisation had swollen its towns and cities. The early
eighteenth century Gothick of Batty Langley and Horace
Walpole was reworked on a grand scale by James Wyatt for the
Prince Regent at Windsor Castle. Gothick forms were swiftly
introduced into chair backs and even fluted cluster-column
legs. Marsh, Tatham and Morel produced furniture on a grand
scale, yet with a playful touch.

CARLTON HOUSE

CARLTON HOUSE was the Prince Regent's sumptuous
London residence. The dining room had a finely-detailed
Gothick ceiling; the pointed-arch motif, with various forms of
crocketting or even rosettes as decoration, were the main
embellishments. The chairs or seating in this style were intended to be light, and were thus often gilt and white or simply
decorated with colour. Regency chiffoniers, with grilled metalwork panels over pleated fabric forming the doors, exist in the
Gothick style and in all the other Ancient styles. Marble tops

Ebonised and gilt octagonal table with Gothic touches, c. 1845.

were also embellished with pierced metalwork galleries and these usually replicated Gothic patterns even if the base of the piece was in another style. By the end of his reign as George IV in 1830, all forms of decoration appeared to have swollen in size as much as the monarch.

MEDIEVAL COPIES

THE REIGN of William IV was characterised by the transition from the light elegance of former styles to a heavy historicism. The nationalistic revival continued, partly as a result of the widespread enthusiasm for the historical romances of Sir Walter Scott, in which the Middle Ages symbolised the golden age of chivalry. Scott's own house, Abbotsford, was part of the passion for restoring early fortified buildings; it was built in the style of a fortified castle, but with the new plate-glass windows and modern comforts.

A widespread interest in genealogy and such forms of early building resulted in a craze for early furniture designs. The many copies and fakes made at the time have a charm and interest of their own, but should not be confused with the real thing. Generally, they remain identifiable from this and later collecting crazes by the remarkable smoothness of all under-surfaces, made by machines or planes, whereas the originals were created with tools such as the adze. Many copies have a variety of old carvings incorporated, for mouldering pieces were retrieved from servants' rooms, barns and other sources. Originals have very worn lower legs, stretchers and feet, whether chairs, stools, cupboards or tables. Anything with sharp edges is suspect. For the early or even late Victorians, this was immaterial: they wanted the look, authentic or not.

A massive mahogany circular dining table, William IV, c. 1835.

Early Victorian

The early Victorians espoused a number of styles, with true Gothic becoming increasingly popular. There were some technical advances, such as the coiled spring, but mass-manufacture threatened a flood of poor-quality furniture. The search for a modern, functional yet innately beautiful style was spearheaded by William Morris.

A CONFUSION OF STYLES

IN THE 1830s several styles developed: a heavy neo-classical one, based on Greek rather than Roman forms; a bogus blown-up Louis XIV style; a Jacobean trend; and also the Gothic, increasingly based on ecclesiastical examples. The Louis styles were applied to chairs, sofas and tables with overblown cabriole legs on pronounced scrolled toes. This was not a revival of the Chippendale style and depended upon white and gilt decoration or the use of walnut, not the walnut of the 1660s to 1740s, but a very curly grained variety with an increasingly dark brown colour as the 1840s passed.

The competition for the rebuilding of the Houses of Parliament (1835) resulted in a famously Gothic winning design, and many pieces of furniture were made in this style, influenced or designed by Augustus Pugin, who used the Christian aspects of Gothic as a triumph over the pagan ones of neo-classicism. Such furniture is often of oak, as is the barley twist Jacobean furniture concurrently popular. All types of wood were used, the best results perhaps being the light ash or sycamore bedroom furniture of the time, subsequently also made in maple and of simple lines.

SIMPLIFIED BEDROOM FURNITURE

BEDROOMS SEEM TO have afforded a welcome release from the historicism of the main rooms of new houses or redecorated old ones. There was also a conscious effort to create hygienic surroundings, and the simple shapes of most bedroom furniture were easily dusted. Large, mirrored-door wardrobes with curving corners are truly Victorian, with large round knobs and handles on the matching chests of drawers. Bedsteads had half-testers and might be of simple mahogany shapes, but by the 1850s metal or brass were increasingly used.

Early Victorian sofa, made from maple wood.

THE COILED SPRING

THE MOST PROFOUND influence on furniture design occurred in the 1830s, with the development of the coiled spring for use in seating stuffing. British rooms were soon transformed by a variety of over-stuffed easy chairs, sofas and day-beds. These were deep-buttoned for extra comfort, but the effect has been likened to a room full of hippopotami. The wooden framework of the seating, already debased by the Louis revival, was now obscured by lavish upholstery and trimmings, just as women's clothes became ever wider as crinoline supports using metal underframes became popular. Attention was directed towards side cabinets with marquetry inlays and carving, much of it machine-made. Dining chairs were also sprung, but many were made on older principles with hooped

A metamorphic library table opening to form steps, c. 1875.

backs, known as balloon backs, and on turned front legs with a kick-out toe. Later versions of the 1840s onwards were more French, with Louis XV cabriole legs.

A comfortable bergère version of this depends upon deep upholstery and short cabriole legs, as does the popular low spoon-back chair with a wider, almost circular, seat. This is popularly thought to have been some form of nursing chair, but was in fact designed for women encumbered by large skirts, so that they could sink and rise gracefully without worrying about chair arms or sides pushing their crinolines into alarming shapes. Similarly, the more rococo forms of side-tables, with contorted cabriole legs, and the popular 'Loo' table – named after a card game – mounted on a central column, allowed for the sweep of these wide skirts.

THE GREAT EXHIBITION

BY 1850 LITTLE progress had been achieved in the invention of a new Victorian style. Papier-mâché chairs, inlaid with mother-of-pearl and painted with birds and flower designs, achieved a moulded appearance as a result of the pressure process by which they were made, but represented a novelty rather than a useful original design. The Great Exhibition of 1851 even featured a sideboard made of gutta-percha (rubber), but was generally condemned for its remarkable paucity of original ideas, and the often nasty way in which factory machinery turned out carvings and parts. A new way forward was sought, also because the sources of mahogany formerly used were virtually exhausted, and later imports from South America lacked the consistent toughness and fine figuring of the early varieties. The finished wood has a more bland orange appearance.

Arts and Crafts

John Ruskin and William Morris were two of the
greatest exponents of the Arts and Crafts ideal.
The latter advocated good craftsmanship and
beauty in every practical object, and an end to
the clutter and mixture of designs that
constituted Victorian taste.

WINDSOR AND SUSSEX CHAIRS

THERE HAD PERSISTED a widespread, locally based
tradition of truly British styles in chair making. The many
forms of these chairs – made of turned parts attached to a solid
shaped seat and known generically now as 'Windsor' chairs –
form a sizeable collectors' field. They used locally available
woods such as beech or elm, and evolved slowly for use in
smaller cottages or the servants' quarters of houses and farms,
for example. William Morris seized on the Sussex chair, a light
armchair with a rush seat, as an example of a simple, practical
form suitable for many locations and fitting his own ideas on
the dignity of honest craftsmanship divorced from the factory.
His famous belief that no one should have anything in their
house unless it is beautiful was the war-cry of a new band of
architects and designers loosely forming what we know as the
Arts and Crafts movement. This was both mocked and seized
upon, for it had become usual by the 1850s to have rooms
in varying styles, rather than having a house made up of just
one style. Different styles were perceived as being appropriate
for certain functions, and furniture designs were applied to
pieces correspondingly.

A Sussex chair: a vernacular style revived successfully by William Morris and produced since the nineteenth century.

ONE STYLE FITS ALL

WILLIAM MORRIS and his consciously reforming
contemporaries were interested in applying a complete style to
architecture and interior design, including furniture. This was
a traditional idea, and fitted their varied philosophies, all
dedicated to removing the stylistic confusion into which mid-
Victorian taste had descended. Oak was a preferred timber, for
the Sussex chair may have been a popular design bought by all
classes for all types of rooms, but it was not typical of the solid
effects sought by many designers, who looked back to the
Middle Ages in an even more romantic manner than Walter
Scott. Supposed 'medieval' forms were adapted to chairs, tables
and all manner of cabinets. The firm of Crace produced some
of the best proportioned and constructed cabinets and many
are in elegant shapes with minimal carving to legs or friezes.
By the 1870s this had become a valid style, but the heavy
religious emphasis was not universally popular. Furthermore,
contrary to intention, the style was favoured by the rich rather
than the poor.

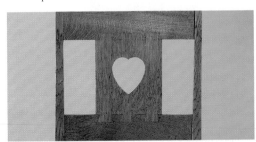

Arts and Crafts chairs made from oak, the preferred timber of the era.

Towards a Simpler Style

New minimalist designers proved too radical for a large home market that was still collecting a variety of diverse styles. However, the 'Cotswold style' found many admirers and began a move towards simple elegance based loosely on straightforward early English medieval designs in English timber, all worked by hand.

FAR EASTERN FASHION

EDWARD GODWIN (1833–86) produced startlingly simple furniture of straight lines, drawing inspiration from Japanese prints, and a new form of Far Eastern decoration emerged. At its most ordinary level this meant bamboo tables with lacquered panels. A wide variety of such furniture was made and forms a distinct collecting area today. It was not produced to fit a complete japonais scheme, but rather as part of the Victorian mania for eclectic, cluttered furnishing – the reverse of the Arts and Crafts ideal, yet also an inspiration for simplification.

A SIMPLER TREND

BY THE 1880s there was a renewed interest in the simpler aspects of the Queen Anne style; red-brick stone-dressed houses with wide windows were popular, fuelling the collecting craze for early furniture of the period, but again only for a few items mixed with other pieces. Nevertheless, the simpler form of architecture was a precursor of the 1890s' designs of Mackmurdo, Voysey and Baillie Scott and the equally adventurous and inventive Mackintosh. Their furniture designs

were of the most simple, angular attenuated form with minimal inlaid decoration, if any. For the British, such revolutionary designs were too extreme, and so little original furniture of this type appears on the market. The influence of these designers on European taste was profound, changing the sinuous Art Nouveau shapes to the geometric lines later favoured.

Ladder-back chair designed by Charles Rennie Mackintosh.

THE COTSWOLD STYLE

IN ENGLAND the more homespun craftsmanship developing in the Cotswolds attracted greater favour. The work of Heal and Barnsley is generally based on a reinterpretation of earlier simple shapes, made by hand of native timbers. Small, rectangular jointed tables are usually of oak, although walnut was popular; chamfered stretchers and usually undecorated surfaces are dependent upon solid timbers, their glorious colour and attractive grain. Reflecting the designs of the late 1660s, elegant cabinets on stands have straightforward bases, even with some holly inlay or other native woods, and bone in the door panels behind which small drawers are fitted. If there is a native style of furniture design, then this has proved a durable one that is still valid today.

Reproduction Furniture

The economic progress of Britain encouraged the factory processes of mass-produced affordable furniture utilising plywood and thin, shiny veneer.

MASS PRODUCTION

THERE ARE STILL quantities of factory-made, cheaply veneered pieces of furniture from the last decades of the nineteenth century and the first decades of the twentieth. The simpler forms by such firms as Maples or Gillow were usually not cheap and have lasted well. From the 1900s until the Second World War, reproductions of former styles became fashionable. The trend towards 'one room, one style' was firmly established during the Edwardian era, with dining rooms in 'eighteenth-century English' and drawing rooms usually in a faux Louis style.

However, after 1900 there was a resurgence of interest in the Adam style and many pieces were made of satinwood (really more Sheraton than Adam). They are distinguished by the attenuated line of their backs and legs, reflecting the furthest continental influence of Art Nouveau. Hepplewhite chairs and sideboards were similarly recreated, but mainly of inferior wood and craftsmanship, instantly recognisable. This style persisted throughout the interwar years and on into the 1950s. It is wise to choose the best, as the machine-made pegged joints that were current by the 1860s are often unstable. The craze for light Louis XVI reproduction furniture was an extension of the 'one room, one style' taste; the 1860s had witnessed a fully over-blown application of machine-made Boulle-work to tables and cabinets with ebonised frames. This latest French craze proves to be more digestible for today's collector, using a piece as a focal point in an otherwise modern interior. Always look for the best quality with doors or drawers that work easily.

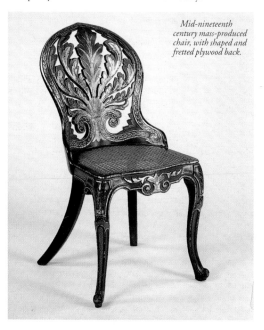

Mid-nineteenth century mass-produced chair, with shaped and fretted plywood back.

Art Deco and Art Moderne

On the Continent, design revolutions – from Bauhaus to Art Moderne – flourished. At home, up-to-date design was used to promote a modern-looking Britain, while behind the front doors of suburban homes, cosiness and comfort were the main considerations.

DESIGN FOR A NEW WORLD

AFTER THE First World War Britain, was largely concerned with rescuing old design forms. But abroad, the 1920s design world was revolutionised by the German Bauhaus, a marriage of industrialisation and Arts and Crafts, and the work of the Swiss designer Le Corbusier, who declared that 'the house is a machine for living in'. Uncompromisingly stark geometric shapes dominated their designs and had some influence in Britain, usually in bastardised form.

Arched mirror framed by open metalwork in a style derived from pre-First World War Austro-German decoration, c. 1928.

The 1925 Paris exhibition of decorative arts was more influential, as it used abstract designs and patterns on furniture still recognisably made in traditional ways, albeit by hand of expensive materials and for the very rich. The later term Art Deco is a 1950s French appellation that is misleading, as it is now also applied to the more streamlined pieces of the 1930s, more correctly termed Art Moderne. The London store Waring and Gillow was prominent in promoting both Art Deco and Moderne furniture made of good materials. The mass-produced furniture still bastardised Antique shapes and styles of all periods, but soon used a form of Art Deco, usually called modernistic or jazz-modern, relying on angular forms and fragmented patterns.

MODERNISM vs SUBURBIA

BY 1930, CERTAIN TRENDS had been absorbed into mainstream furniture design. Easy chairs and sofas were made with wide arms and slab-like backs and seats. Characteristically, a wide variety of small tables could be low and round or of octagonal shape. The firm of Heals also sold modernistic furniture, including some designs by Gordon Russell, who also designed wireless sets. The development of bent-plywood, used extensively in factory made furniture from the 1860s, was refined and even applied to bentwood chairs. At this time tubular steel furniture was mass produced by the British company PEL, and although little was sold for domestic interiors it became a familiar sight in shops, restaurants or hotels – in fact anywhere efficient, clean lines seemed appropriate. The chromed finish was more suitable for commercial premises, as it offended the British taste for cosy domesticity, exemplified by the ever-growing suburbs all over Britain.

The 1930s

MANY mass-produced 1930s items are highly collectable, and the advent of early plastics and new technology such as wireless sets pushed design in new directions. However, hand-made furniture was still being made to the highest standards.

MASS PRODUCTION BETWEEN THE WARS

THE BEST and longest-lived designs are undoubtedly those following the example of the Cotswold school, simplified for inter-war tastes. Much of the amusing Moderne furniture of that time has vanished; it was a short-lived style and was never made to last. Better collectable pieces include cocktail cabinets, radiograms, sideboards and bedroom furniture. Many large dressing tables with circular or shaped mirrors can be found. Look for the pale woods if you want an authentic period touch; the best always had a matching stool. Because most were made of thin plywood with a veneer, it is often the case that drawers are badly fitting. The better-made products are from Hille,

Heals, Maples and Waring and Gillow, and are correspondingly more expensive. Other typical products of the period include tea-trolleys, magazine racks and fitted kitchen cabinets, modern

Easy chair made of tubular steel and leather, dating from c. 1932.

forms of the dressers used in kitchens since the Middle Ages.
English Rose began producing metal cabinets in the mid-1930s
and these can still be found.

BETTY JOEL

THIS WAS A PERIOD when items could still be commissioned and hand made. The name of the Betty Joel factory is
symbolic of the best of true 1930s design. David Joel had
learned about plys and glues by studying boat-building, and his
wife Betty collected Oriental porcelain, so the curves and
simple geometric shapes of their furniture designs are modern,
but have a timeless quality. They are now expensive, because
apart from being well-made and proportioned, they also use
unusual woods as veneers, brought from all over the old British
Empire. Most of the timbers used by the Betty Joel factory are
now virtually impossible to find. Their furniture stands alone as
distinctively of its period and should be regarded as a yardstick
in design.

EARLY PLASTICS

EARLY BAKELITE and plastics form another collecting field
and were mainly used for knobs and handles, although lamps,
especially standard lamps and some table-bases had supports of
translucent plastics. These are known to be unstable now, so
check for areas of softness that indicate decay. The most famous
icon of inter-war furniture is undoubtedly the wireless set in all
its varieties. 'EKCO' produced the famous circular black
phenolite Wells Coates set in the mid-1930s, and together with
the telephone of that date form a must for those fascinated by
the period. As with all pieces from the inter-war years, buy the
most pristine examples.

Utility Furniture

The simplicity demanded by the rationing of furnishing materials extended a design trend started before the Second World War. By the 1950s, metal was used to produce light, strong furniture, and space-saving fitted furniture became popular.

WARTIME RATIONING

THE SECOND WORLD WAR of 1939–45 was not a totally inactive period for the furniture designer. Although furniture production was soon rationed, design of Utility pieces (approved by the government to conform to strict rationing of resources and labour) was overseen by Gordon Russell, who had pioneered lighter modern furniture, including the slim streamlined upholstered easy chair, by 1938. His experience of traditional and modern techniques and design resulted in very simple Cotswold school-inspired designs using native woods. Simple chairs with matching tables were in truth an extension of the most basic pre-war designs.

The development of the horizontal wide spring for chair seats in Germany had been used in Knoll chairs and the open arms and padded back with simple sprung seat cushion

Laminated bentwood, combined arm and leg component for a light, open armchair, dating from 1938.

were as useful in the house as in the motor car design
influencing them. Many developments in plastics and
metallurgy were applied to furniture production after the
war, together with improved glues and plywood production.

METAL SUPPORTS

UNTIL 1953 there were still restrictions on the use of materials
and most goods were exported to recoup wartime expenses. By
1951, young designers such as Ernest Race and Robin Day had
evolved light metal constructions for chairs and tables. The legs
of pieces from such modern designers had a raked tapering line,
fine in steel or aluminium, but structurally weak when
replicated in wood. But the style was widespread; the low coffee
table, a symbol of the 1950s, especially in teak, sold as a
Scandinavian-inspired design influence. By the 1960s, legs were
turned and tapering, often still raked and capped by brass.

FITTED CUPBOARDS

FORMICA AND PLASTICS were mainly confined to the
kitchen, and many tables or trolleys are of cheerful form and
colour. The traditional Windsor chair was restyled by the firm of
Ercol to form low arm and side chairs, even settees, with cushions.
This furniture is now unusual as it was made of solid wood, a
dwindling resource. The desire for light furniture was also affected
by the increasing use of fitted cabinets and wardrobes, so that
spaces appeared uncluttered except for one or two antique items.
The craze for collecting antiques had been fuelled by post-war
shortages, and in the 1950s Victorian and Edwardian furniture was
regularly cut down to make smaller useful items. The collecting of
Victorian smaller pieces was popular, as spoon-back chairs took up
little space and fitted in with the lighter look.

The 1960s to Today

THE 1960s were a period of great experiments with plastic and paper furniture, in which Italy led the way. Although widely illustrated in British design journals, plastic chairs of translucent, vibrantly coloured inflatable designs were novelties, finding few commercial outlets in Britain.

TERENCE CONRAN

THE MOST FAMOUS design success of the 1960s was initiated by Terence Conran, with his 'Habitat' styles. Trained as a designer, Conran worked on the Festival of Britain and then had a brief career as a fabric and ceramic designer. His own shop specialised in metal furniture. Habitat produced versions of tubular steel split-cane seated chairs and wooden furniture clearly derived from Bauhaus examples, then enjoying great popularity in a Germany reacting against its Nazi past. Such chairs were relatively well made and are worth collecting as their simple outline has a timeless elegance. Check joints and seats, as repairs can be expensive.

MECHANISED ITEMS

THE 1950s AND 1960s were a period of excitement in the development of household gadgets, and there is a thriving market for these. Anything with a case, such as radio, television or stereogram is likely to be well made of good materials. The PYE 'Black Box' is an example of an early stereo record player finished to a high standard and marking the end of 300 years of British fascination with Oriental furniture forms, the curved shape lacquered black and decorated with chinoiserie designs. Similarly, some of the 1950s' television cabinets with the cabriole legs and double doors are redolent of earlier forms of furniture-making. The expense of creating such an absurdity today makes such items of interest, for few remain intact.

There are still furniture-makers alive working in traditional ways, such as John Makepeace, and their work is collected. Unlike their predecessors, it is arguably not typical of its period, as the style is uniquely that of the maker, unreflective of other 'fashionable' transient styles. Such items are usually commissioned for a specific purpose and if they appear on the market can command large sums. It seems as though such items will be the most sought-after antiques of the future.

The fashionably turned and tapering stiletto leg of a 'coffee table' in its heyday, c. 1960.

IDENTIFYING FURNITURE
ARMS

FROM DENOTING the symbolic existence of a chair as the expression of the power of the owner, the armchair became associated with comfort and elegantly strong construction.

Egyptian, New Kingdom (18th Dynasty) c. 1330 BC
Very rare surviving piece of symbolism in chair arm design, from Tutankhamen's throne: feathered wings and iconographic carving covered with gold leaf as evidence of sophistication thousands of years ago.

  1330 BC **p. 13**

George III, English c. 1780
Graeco-Roman civilisation revived with carved gessoed giltwood spiral twist and foliate arm supports with padded rests.

   1780 **p. 59**

Edward I, English c. 1296
*Coronation Chair of Edward I. Downswept
arm above solid oak construction with infill of
arched carved Gothic design. Originally
painted and gilt, reflecting the
surrounding architecture.*

George III, English c. 1790
*Attenuated arm and integrated
front support giving a flowing
line to a painted and gilt
beechwood chair.*

Tudor, English
c. 1550
Shaped oak arm and baluster turned support. The notched decoration enabled the tying of soft cushions to the frame.

  p. 22

Regency, English c. 1810
Ebonised and gilt beechwood chair arm and support, with leopard's head and anthemion design inspired by Antique Greek examples revived by Thomas Hope et al.

  p. 64

George III, English c. 1790
Carved moulded mahogany
show-wood frame and
upholstered elbow/arm pad of a
settee, with fluted shaped arm rest
and carved details.

George III, English c. 1790
Downswept ebonised and gilt arm and
turned rest of beechwood chair.

George III, English
c. 1755
Needlework upholstered arm/elbow pad with scrolled support in mahogany.

George II, English
c. 1745
Shaped mahogany arm with under-scrolled and swept back support enabling an arrangement of the then-fashionable large skirts of dresses and coats.

George III, English
c. 1775
Upholstered armchair arm with
a carved hand rest and a scrolled
moulded support.

George III, English
c. 1775
Sophisticated carved wooden arm
with gilt gesso and moulded
scrolled carving supporting a
small upholstered elbow rest.

George III, English c. 1790
Delicately modelled carved gilt gesso and off-white decorated downswept arm, typical of the Adam period. The shape accommodated the elaborately skirted clothes of men and women.

Regency, English c. 1815
Downswept and under-scrolled mahogany arm modelled on Antique Grecian designs, the flamboyant elaboration of the carved acanthus leaf and ormolu mounts typical of the high fashion of the day.

Regency, English
c. 1810
Neo-Grecian over-scrolled arm of
a chaise longue, copied directly
from Antique sculpted examples.
Painted decoration resembling
rosewood and ormolu mounts.
Delicate elegance.

Regency, English
c. 1815
Emulating Graeco-Roman
Antique sculptured thrones, the
scrolled arm-supports of this
upholstered chair are embellished
with neoclassical foliate
decorative motifs.

Victorian, English c. 1880
Solid shaped oak on a gondola-shaped 'folding 'x'-frame chair of oak. One of the oldest designs for a simple portable chair updated.

Regency, English c. 1815
Revival of the design for a 'folding' x-framed chair of painted and gilt beechwood with a delicate framework that is immovable, except when the legs break across the grain. A rare survival of an extreme style for the very rich.

Arts and Crafts, English c. 1880
Echoes of the Ancient x-frame chair in the shape of the arm of this Sussex chair. A vernacular style revived successfully by William Morris and produced since the nineteenth century.

BACKS

ONCE TREATED as mere supports or draughtshields,
the back of a chair or settee became a display of the carver
and craftsman's skills. This also reflected the taste and
affluence of the owner.

Edward I, English c. 1296
Coronation Chair of Edward I: solidity
and power inherent in the forceful design
and oak construction, utilising a Gothic
back derived from ecclesiastical
architecture of the period, yet based on
Roman and Carolingian examples.

Tudor, English c. 1550
Basic structures of solid carved oak have
survived relatively well and the local or
vernacular tradition altered little over the
centuries. Leaves, roses and foliage
delineate an elaborate example.

*Charles II, English
c. 1680
Profusely carved seventeenth-
century walnut examples,
displaying Dutch influences,
with turned walnut frame-
work, which would have
replicated that of the seats.*

George III, English
c. 1760
Slender mahogany framework of
'Oriental' or Chinese inspiration,
for an airy open armchair
intended for an informal setting.

p. 42

George III, English c. 1775
Square mahogany back of a hall chair
with a dished mahogany seat, the
central circle with a sun-ray device
incorporating an armorial panel .

p. 42

George III, English c. 1795
Armchair back with the refinement of a design eliminating all superfluous detail, with a curved split-cane infilled back-rest with integrated arms, arm-rests and legs.

George III, English c. 1790
Based on a French Louis XVI design for a bergère, with carved giltwood front arm-rest, all details adapted from neoclassical sources.

**Arts and Crafts, English
c. 1880**
*Turned beech frame of a
vernacular open armchair; a
refined design of the famous
Sussex chair popularised by
William Morris.*

  1880 **p. 80**

**Arts and Crafts,
English c. 1895**
*Simple but attenuated square
tapering oak back framework,
with shaped horizontal backsplats embracing a pierced
fretwork heart motif – a
particularly favourite device of
the architect and designer
C. A. Voysey.*

 1895 **p. 84**

George I, English
c. 1725
Shaped japanned back with 'Oriental' designs, incorporating a distinctive scroll device based on a Chinese original.

1725　p. 42

Queen Anne, English
c. 1710
Elaborately shaped walnut veneered shaped back with a central vase-shaped stylised motif lending a rococo silhouette to the back uprights, extensions of the legs.

1710　p. 38

George I, English c. 1715
Simplified variant of a shaped walnut veneered side chair back incorporating strong 'c' scroll motifs around the central vase-shaped splat.

Queen Anne, English c. 1710
Upholstered back to a walnut armchair with an outline clearly defining the open wooden styles of the time and covered in needlework.

George II, English
c. 1755
*Typical squared back to a practical
and comfortable upholstered wide
chair, used in libraries or less formal
settings. This one tightly covered
with needlework. Made by all
cabinet-makers.*

George II, English
c. 1745
*Squared lines softened by the use
of a camel or humped-backed
line to the top-rail, also forming a
useful head rest. A more
sophisticated touch reminiscent of
the back design of wing chairs.*

George II, English c. 1745
Mahogany framed side-chair,
with an elaborately carved back
utilising rococo 'c' scrolls and a
bold variant of both shell and leaf
motifs.

George II, English c. 1755
Attenuated lines of a robustly framed
and shaped mahogany armchair back,
incorporating open-fret backsplat
derived from the earlier vase shape.

George II, English
c. 1755
Advanced inverted vase design of an open-fret carved back with Gothic motifs, incorporated into subtly shaped uprights and top-rail.

George II, English
c. 1755
Lively use of the rococo and popular Gothic themes adapted to crisply carved tough mahogany furniture; the playful circle and shell motif on the top-rail display the virtuosity of the carver creating a minor work of art.

George III, English
c. 1765
Cartouche-shaped carved
mahogany side-chair back, with
three carved and pierced
backsplats incorporating
neoclassical details and the
top-rail with foliate carving.

George III, English
c. 1770
Mahogany armchair with a
cartouche-shaped back,
incorporating carved neoclassical
details centred on an urn and
inverted pierced anthemion leaf.

George III, English
c. 1775
Upholstered cartouche-shaped back to an open mahogany armchair, the dished curves of the back echoing the shape of the seat.

George III, English
c. 1795
Typical shield back to an armchair of beechwood, with an off-white and gilt decoration, the remarkably slim outline of the back tightly upholstered.

George III, English
c. 1790
Shaped pierced beechwood armchair back with a split-cane panel surrounded by ebonised and gilt decoration, the swept arms emanating from the top of the back support.

Regency, English c. 1810
Typically scrolled and swept outline to a gilt and ebonised beechwood armchair, incorporating incised neoclassical decoration, a split-cane panel and a turned curved horizontal support for comfort.

George III, English c. 1800
The height of Georgian neoclassical-inspired elegance, with a scrolled outline and 'x'-shaped back-rest, ebonised and gilt beechwood with finely painted panel to the decorated turned top-rail.

Regency, English c. 1815
Boldly shaped and decorated back-rest of neoclassical inspiration, set between typically scrolled supports of the ebonised and gilt beechwood frame.

Regency, English c. 1820
*Elaborately carved and shaped
mahogany framed split-cane infilled
bergère armchair, based on powerful
Antique examples, softened with loose
cushions and given importance with
the fine ormolu mounts of rosettes
and anthemions.*

   1820 **p. 66**

Regency, English c. 1825
*Scrolled tub outline of an upholstered
luxurious armchair based on Antique
Roman thrones seen in carvings;
typical 'High' Regency.*

    1825 **p. 71**

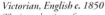

Victorian, English c. 1850
*The introduction of mass-produced coiled
springs, distinct from hand-made ones,
influenced the form of easy chairs: strong
frames partially hidden by the deep
upholstery, usually buttoned, and
strong small legs.*

    1850 **p. 78**

Regency, English c. 1810

A 'Klismos' chair, directly copied from Antique pots or carved sources, is modernised by an infilled back of double-sided split-caned panelling.

Victorian, English c. 1855

Machine-made and mass-produced furniture increasingly dominated nineteenth-century furniture-making. Glued thin sheets of steam-pressed ply-wood could be shaped and fretted to suit many purposes, as with this chair back.

Elizabeth II, English c. 1955

Bent-hooped back of beechwood with turned upright supports, fitting as dowels into the shaped solid seat. An updated vernacular design, as used worldwide in the 1950s.

George VI, English c. 1950
The full panoply of mechanised
furniture-making techniques: steam-
bent and shaped ply frame, with
similarly shaped upright springy back-
rest of a light wood, usually birch
or beech.

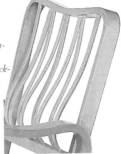

George VI, English
c. 1950
Chair back of utilitarian design,
the form allowing the use of loose
cushions for padding and adapting
to the shape of the individual body.
Simple construction treated as an
aesthetic exercise.

CARVINGS
AND MOULDINGS

OFTEN OF deep symbolic significance to the craftsman and
patron, the decoration of a piece of furniture is not simply
indicative of its date: details are forms of cryptography.

Egypt, New Kingdom (18th Dynasty)
c. 1330 BC
Carved polychrome decoration forming
winged and other symbols used in
Ancient Egypt and subsequently adapted
for other civilisations including our own.
From Tutankhamen's throne.

    1330 BC   p. 13

Regency, English
c. 1810
Winged draped carved giltwood and
ebonised decorative female form as a
caryatid on a cabinet, influenced by
archaeological discoveries in the
wake of the Napoleonic Wars.

   1810 p. 66

Regency, English c. 1810
Carved animals' heads and anthemion underline the importance of Antique influences and Classical learning in civilised society of the period.

Regency, English c. 1815
Stars, balls and rope motifs indicate both neoclassical Graeco-Roman and Egyptian influences, updated to Britain's victorious defeat of Napoleon and used for the frame of a convex mirror.

Regency, English c. 1815

Lion's, leopard's, ram's and eagle's feet derived from Antique Greek, Roman and Egyptian carefully researched originals, often blended or reinvented by the major craftsmen of the day. Chair foot with foliate motif.

1815   p. 70

George III, English c. 1790

Spiral twisted columnar giltwood carved support with neoclassical supporting motifs facing the front arm-rest of a bergère chair.

1790   p. 62

Regency, English c. 1815
*Cast and chased ormolu
(gilt bronze) decorative mount
derived from Grecian examples
and a design of Thomas Hope on a
refined rosewood chiffonier.*

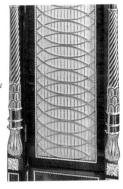

George III, English c. 1780
*Carved giltwood ram's heads and
ebonised serpents representing the
Classical Caduceus of Mercury,
decorating a neoclassical torchère
based upon Ancient Greek
examples from the Temple of Apollo
at Delphi. Such torchères were
intended to hold candelabra.*

George III, English c. 1780

Typical decorative scrolled arm terminal, carved giltwood with neoclassical foliate design relating to the overall design of the legs and back.

 1780 p. 59

George I, English c. 1725

Imposingly carved giltwood cabriole leg with motifs based on Antique Roman examples, with large naturalistic hairy paw foot. Cartouche and other carving typically Baroque.

    1725 p. 40

Regency, English c. 1810
Ormolu mounts used on mahogany furniture were fashionable symbols of luxury. Neoclassical rosettes, anthemions and palmettes were consistently popular, as on this chair.

Regency, English c. 1815
Carved giltwood decoration on an overmantel, with putty-coloured ground reflecting various neoclassical motifs and the 'musket ball' referring to British victories abroad.

George III, English c. 1785

A carved giltwood wall-bracket with neoclassical decoration of palm and acanthus leaves terminating in fruit motifs.

Regency, English c. 1815

A typically carved giltwood convex mirror with neoclassical trophies of war and victory epitomised by the eagle cresting and musket balls: topical references to the Napoleonic Wars.

George I, English c. 1720
Carved giltwood frieze of an early eighteenth-century side or console table with massive related swags, leaves and a central shell in the Antique taste of William Kent.

George I, English c. 1725
Carved giltwood table frieze with Vitruvian scroll decoration and a double shell motif with typical leafy carving. A reflection of the Venetian and Roman inspiration drawn on by such designers as William Kent.

Queen Anne, English
c. 1705

Carved giltwood and gesso leafy cresting and decorative cornice of a sophisticated early mirror frame with a typically flat profile.

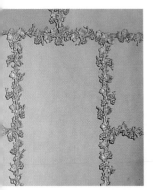

George III, English
c. 1770

Delicately carved decorative giltwood trailing carving, subdividing the enormous expanse of a large mirror.

George III, English c. 1760
Flamboyant rococo carved giltwood bracket with leafy 'c' scrolls, rocaille (rock and shell) decoration popularly associated with Thomas Chippendale's designs.

    1760 *p. 46*

George II, English c. 1755
Carved giltwood and gesso cornice and eagle cresting of a rococo mirror frame including leafy 'c' scrolls, rocaille decoration and unusual use of strapwork, originally popular in Elizabethan architecture.

 1755 *p. 50*

George II, English c. 1730
Attenuated carved giltwood and gesso wall bracket with rocaille decoration, stylised flower-heads and leaves.

George II, English c. 1745
Elaborately carved giltwood mirror frame cornice with a swans'-neck cresting enriched by 'diamond panes' and rococo foliate and leafy carvings in the manner of the designer Abraham Swan.

George I, English c. 1715
Decorative carved giltwood cartouche
and cresting with neoclassical egg and
dart moulding above decorative shell
motif.

Tudor, English c. 1545
Pierced arched Gothic tracery decorating an early side table-cupboard providing ventilated food storage.

 1545 p. 18

Elizabethan, English c. 1560
Quatrefoil and arched Gothic carved tracery motifs enclosed by circles and half-round carvings of an oak frieze of a chair back.

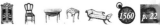 1560 p. 22

Tudor, English c. 1540

Carved oak armchair back with panelled construction and a shaped cresting. Carved arched enclosed motif encompassing the Tudor rose.

   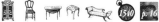   1540   p. 16

Charles II, English c. 1680

Oak armchair back carved with stylised artichoke flower-head and associated foliage with rose-heads in a decorative running pattern border.

       1680   p. 27

Charles II, English
c. 1680
*Carved ebonised beechwood legs
and a foliate carved pierced
arched stretcher, derived from
Daniel Marot's designs.*

1680 p. 31

Charles II, English
c. 1680
*Turned walnut legs and lower
stretchers enhanced by carved
pierced stretchers utilising variou.
foliate forms considered typically
English.*

1680 p.

Queen Anne, English c. 1710

Shaped curving knee of a walnut cabriole leg, enhanced by carved scrolled ears.

George II, English c. 1755

Intricately carved knee of a mahogany cabriole leg, decorated with clustered acanthus leaves, marrying rococo and neoclassical details.

p. 40

George I, English
c. 1725

Neoclassical carved shell and acanthus leaf motifs used in a free manner on the cresting of a mahogany chair back.

George II, English
c. 1740

Double eagle-headed motif forming the cresting of a mahogany chair back. Freely adapted neoclassical motif above pierced vase-shaped centre splat.

George III, English
c. 1770
Shaped, carved and moulded
mahogany chair back with
pierced splats, neoclassical
paterae and rococo floral motifs.

   p. 54

George III, English
c. 1770
Pierced, shaped back of a
mahogany hall chair
incorporating a family crest,
neoclassical acanthus leaf and
'drapery' as tassels.

    p. 54

***George III, English
c. 1780***
*Carved, pierced backsplat and
frame of a mahogany chair,
embodying English neoclassicism
with foliate cresting and
acanthus leaf centred by an urn.*

Regency, English c. 1815
*Painted or simulated wooden
back of a chair decorated with
gilt neoclassical decoration of
acanthus leaves and shell
motif cresting.*

George III, English
c. 1765
Neoclassical swan's-neck broken
pediment with pierced and carved
open-fret cresting; Gothic style
enhanced by carved rosettes and dentil
decoration.

George III, English
c. 1765
Mahogany swan's-neck broken
pediment, with decorative pierced
open-fret cresting; Chinese or
'Oriental' design merging Gothic leaf
patterns in corners.

George III, English c. 1770
Typical carved and fluted frieze of mahogany adapted from neoclassical examples.

Regency, English c. 1815
Carved and open-fret frieze and sides to a jardinière showing 'Oriental' influences akin to Moghul or Indian inspired styles of the period best seen at the Brighton Pavilion.

William and Mary, English
c. 1695
Turned walnut finial derived from
neoclassical sources – urns and
vases – and applied to the cresting
of a 'double domed' bureau
bookcase.

William and Mary, English
c. 1700
Japanned and lacquered drawer
fronts in the 'Chinoiserie' manner,
inspired by authentic Far Eastern
examples of lacquer or porcelain.

George III, English c. 1790
Painted and gilt decoration of a chair frame, with neoclassical rosette and painted bands imitating the moulded decoration of more expensive chairs.

George III, English c. 1790
Neoclassical turned, carved and fluted decorative split pilasters imitating end legs or supports, applied to a chiffonier door.

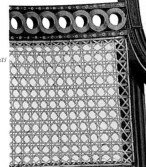

George III, English c. 1790
Rectangular caned chair back
with circular pierced design
outlined in painted decoration as
a neoclassical guilloche pattern
on simulated ebony ground.

   1790 p. 54

Victorian, English c. 1875
Carved panel depicting tropical
foliage in a carved frame, typical
of nineteenth-century Imperial
British taste.

  1875 p. 79

FEET AND CASTERS

THE STYLE of a foot reveals more than its age and speaks of the taste of the original owner; it indicates current preoccupations, while casters depict advancing technology.

Egyptian, New Kingdom (18th Dynasty) c. 1330 BC
Giltwood carved lion's paw foot with highlighted ebonised claws on a tiny turned support, from the tomb of Tutankhamen.

Regency, English c. 1810
Supporting leg of a stand for a box, inspired by Ancient Egyptian archeological discoveries in the wake of the Napoleonic Wars.

Regency, English c. 1815
Naturalistic form of lion's paw foot on the sleek ebonised frame of an open armchair.

Regency, English c. 1820
Ancient Rome recalled in an expressively modelled lion's paw foot of giltwood for an imposing throne-like tub chair.

 1820   p. 70

George II, English c. 1740
Early eighteenth-century, Roman-inspired, 'antique' carved giltwood lion's paw foot, reminiscent of Kent.

 1740   p. 40

George I, English c. 1725
Stylised elegance in the form of a squared, naturalistically carved, walnut paw foot, symbolising familiarity with the Classical tradition.

 1725   p. 38

George I, English c. 1715
Attenuated leg with naturalistic hairy paw foot of domestic beast rather than a predator, referring to a domestic view of Antiquity.

 1715   p. 40

George I, English c. 1715
Carved walnut claw-and-ball foot familiar from religious use as a lectern base in church, adapted from Ancient Rome.

George I, English c. 1720
Symbolism blended with technology: claw-and-ball foot fitted with a caster, uniting past and present with a clear sculptural technique.

George I, English c. 1725
Another version of the claw-and-ball foot attached to a shaped, attenuated cabriole leg.

George I, English c. 1725
Intricately carved and shaped domesticated claw-and-ball foot, with a well-defined display of sheathed claws concealing a brass caster.

Queen Anne, English c. 1710
Less aggressive form of 'modern' foot of the period: the pad foot as a rational alternative for simpler settings, taking the shape of the leg on a giltwood centre table.

    *1710* **p. 40**

Queen Anne, English c. 1710
Dynamically shaped, short cabriole leg and worled disc pad foot.

 *1710* **p. 40**

Queen Anne, English c. 1710
Slight cabriole form to a walnut leg with a fatter profile to match.

 *1710* **p. 38**

George I, English c. 1720
A form of double foot is visible at the base of a subtle cabriole form and a slimmer pad is achieved visually by carving the bulk of it at the base.

     1720 **p. 40**

William and Mary, English c. 1700
Inlaid walnut torchère on a tripod base, composed of elegant 's' scrolls derived from fashionable baroque examples of the period.

George III, English c. 1765
Pointed club foot of the mahogany tripod base of a dished-top, small centre table.

Queen Anne, English c. 1710
A walnut, leafy carved, pad foot, showing the novelty embellishment of a plain walnut design.

George I, English c. 1715
Various forms of the pad foot were utilised
during the early eighteenth century, including
rare lacquered or japanned ones. Oriental motifs
were adapted for English or European tastes on
characteristically English legs.

      1715 **p. 31**

George II, English c. 1750
Outswept simulated pad foot with a
slender profile epitomising the waning
of its popularity.

1750 **p. 46**

George III, English c. 1770
Outswept foot on a tiny shaped support, the
acanthus leaf carving embodying both rococo
and neoclassical taste.

1770 **p. 50**

Charles II, English c. 1680

Nature was the inspiration for cabinet-makers and carvers; a source for this leafy carved foot on a turned leg. Termed a 'Braganza' toe after the wife of Charles II.

     1680 p. 29

George III, English c. 1770

Dashingly slender profile to a carved cabriole leg, terminating in a light, naturalistic scroll toe, which was much popularised by Thomas Chippendale's designs.

    1770 p. 46

George III, English c. 1775

Crisply carved profile, enabled by the use of high-quality close-grained mahogany. The scroll toe is embellished with a carved acanthus leaf.

     1775 p. 54

George III, English c. 1770

Scroll toe, flamboyantly carved in imitation of natural wood shapes, but creating an illusion of great artifice by using a thin moulded mahogany cabriole leg.

     1770 p. 54

George III, English c. 1780
Simple turned and fluted leg of neoclassical inspiration, given a ring turning to the tapered terminal beneath.

     1780 p. 54

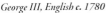

George III, English c. 1780
Carved, turned, gilt beechwood chair leg.

     1780 p. 54

George III, English c. 1785
Variant of the use of carving and gilding to a chair leg: coloured gesso with gilding, demonstrated by Adam.

    1785 p. 54

George III, English c. 1760
Robust neoclassicism mingled with Gothic fantasy: a cluster-column mahogany leg, carved with great artistry.

      1760 p. 48

George III, English c. 1775
Simple use of carved, turned mahogany, with shaped toe further lightening an airy design for an armchair.

      1775 p. 54

Regency, English c. 1825
Neoclassicism studied and distilled into a turned leg of attenuated 'melon' form, further decorated with convex flutings and ring turnings. A complicated fashion for reviving old forms.

    1825 p. 72

George III, English c. 1770
'Classic' example of neoclassicism. A turned beechwood leg, turned and carved then fluted and given a turned toe.

   1770 p. 54

George III, English c. 1770
Slender version of elaborate gilt examples of fluted, turned legs; in this case mahogany enhanced by a carved disc turning.

     1770 p. 54

George III, English c. 1785
Baluster turned, mahogany foot, reminiscent of seventeenth-century examples, but in fact a fashionably sophisticated reference to surviving vernacular styles.

   1785 p. 54

George II, English c. 1730
Bracket feet obviate a heavy plinth base and add lightness to the superstructures outline. A pine foot veneered with burr walnut emphasising the elaborate construction of an otherwise simple outline.

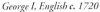

George I, English c. 1720
A variant of a bracket foot, with simple outline curving to a point enhancing the angle of the veneered superstructure and integrated foot.

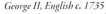

George II, English c. 1735
Yewwood veneers on a simple foot reflect the veneers used on the carcase of the bureau, emphasising the physical unity of the piece.

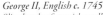

George II, English c. 1745
Slim bracket foot with scrolled angle support emphasising the quality of veneers and colour of the piece.

Regency, English c. 1810
Shaped beechwood, outswept or sabre leg drawing on Antique sources. Now so termed because of the period of its greatest popularity during the Napoleonic Wars and the great British land and sea victories. Typically ebonised with gilt decoration.

    1810 *p. 66*

Regency, English c. 1820
Shaped foot resembling a scythe or scimitar, embodying updated Antique designs executed in mahogany.

    1820 *p. 70*

George III, English c. 1790
A simple, unaffected design with timeless straight lines, but clearly neoclassical in inspiration utilising ebonised, gilt-enhanced decoration.

    *1790* *p. 54*

George III, English c. 1785
Cut-away plinth design of a secretaire bookcase with angled and curved outline suggesting Antique influences.

   1785 *p. 54*

George III, English c. 1785
Elegantly tapered, slim lines highlighted by the thicker detail at the base of the leg forming the toe.

     *1785* *p. 54*

George III, English c. 1785
Elaborately moulded, square, tapering mahogany chair leg with stepped, spaced toe block lending decoration and vital strength.

     *1785* *p. 54*

George III, English c. 1790
Spade toe with darker colour emphasising the base of the lighter, square, tapering, slim leg utilising an expensively exotic wood, satinwood.

    *1790* *p. 58*

George III, English c. 1790
Strong foot designed as an enlarged spade toe, but given a lighter profile with decorative borders of contrasting colour and wood. The shape is a pared down version of a neoclassical design.

    1790 *p. 58*

William and Mary, English c. 1690

The famous 'bun' foot of the late seventeenth and early eighteenth centuries; a lighter version of European Baroque variants, and an inflated version of a bobbin turning.

  1690 p. 34

Regency, English c. 1825

Lotus foot symptomatic of advanced studies of Antique design, but also influenced by British possessions in the Far East and India. Here carved in exotic rosewood and concealing a caster beneath the petals.

   1825 p. 64

William and Mary, English c. 1690

Neoclassical acanthus leaf enhancing the foot of an ebonised, carved beechwood stool.

    1690 p. 29

Regency, English c. 1825

Ormolu cast foot of a tripod base for a music stand with acanthus and lion's paw foot decoration.

   1825 p. 64

George III, English c. 1760

Evolution of the caster forms a study in industrial progress. This early version has sections of tough leather compressed over a brass rod enabling mobility without damaging fine wood floors.

 1760 p. 50

George III, English c. 1785

Elegantly designed tapering, square leg with a spade toe fitted into a tight brass cap and strong caster.

    1785 p. 48

George II, English c. 1755

Moulded chamfered, straight mahogany leg with leather castor acting as a roller on hardwood floors.

    1755 p. 42

George III, English c. 1790

Outswept, reeded, tapering foot of a table fitted with a decorative and utilitarian brass cap above the caster.

    1790 p. 54

Regency, English c. 1820

Casters indicate the fluid room arrangements and multiple use accorded to much furniture during the Regency period; this turned tapered chair leg and brass caster are utilitarian, but also decorative.

George III, English c. 1785

Turned, fluted, satinwood leg with a discrete caster within the terminal of the foot.

George III, English c. 1785

Square capped caster for a moulded leg terminating in a spade toe with a defining collar.

George III, English c. 1800

Typically composed lion's paw foot, here terminating in a caster.

George III, English c. 1795
Outswept leg with a brass capped toe and a caster as an extension of the decoration of the foot.

  *p. 60*

Late Regency, English c. 1830
Turned and tapered leg of Antique Greek inspiration with an ormolu capped foot and a large caster.

    *p. 70*

Late Regency, English c. 1830
Industrialisation now applied to components of furniture on a large scale. This decorative spoked wheel is an elegant design enhancing the practical purpose of a two-tier buffet.

   p. 72

William IV, English c. 1835
Ormolu caster with a melon neoclassical motif on the toe attachment of a short-legged chair.

    *p. 74*

Regency, English c. 1830
Elaborately detailed foot with a small caster ensuring mobility on a carpeted floor.

Regency, English c. 1810
Melon-shaped carved motif giltwood toe with an ormolu foot on an imposing Canterbury.

Regency, English c. 1810
Brass casters on a double capped, melon carved motif toe forming rosewood and gilt embellishments.

William IV, English c. 1835
Unusual design replicating a beehive and used as a foot for a massively heavy circular dining table; the foot also houses solid casters.

HANDLES

HANDLES REVEAL the advancing technical skills of a cabinet-maker, the fashions of the period and decorative devices favoured by the educated.

William and Mary, English c. 1695
Early decorative form of brass drop handle and back-plate.

    1695 **p. 34**

Charles II to Queen Anne, English c. 1660–1710
Simple, baluster-shaped, brass drop handle with moulded outline to the back-plate.

    1660 **p. 28**

Charles II to Queen Anne, English c. 1680–1720
Decorative back-plate and flatter baluster drop.

   1680 **p. 28**

Queen Anne to George II, English c. 1700–1730
Pierced brass, flat back-plate with elegant cartouche outline and simple handle.

    1700 **p. 28**

George II, English c. 1740

Typical early Georgian solid brass, cartouche shaped, back-plate of brass with a pierced keyhole.

George III, English c. 1765

Elaborately cast back-plate with rococo details and wider profiled handle. Such fittings were often gilt to enhance the chasing and the contrasts with the fine timbers on which they were used.

George II to George III, English c. 1740–1800

Standard form of brass handle and simple pommel used from about 1740 to 1800, mainly on mahogany furniture and often gilt when used on finer pieces, usually mahogany.

George II to George III, English c. 1740–1800

Elaborate version of the simple swan's-neck handle design, but with a central piece of decoration.

George II to George III, English c. 1740–1800
Simple handle placed to great effect as a contrast to the
grain of the wood and set with a keyhole centrally
positioned above.

 p. 42

George II to George III, English c. 1740–1800
Oval panel emphasising the curves of an elegantly
shaped curving handle and decorative pommels.

 p. 42

George III, English c. 1760
Simple outline elaborately detailed with continental
rococo details and gilt for maximum impact.

 p. 45

George III, English c. 1765
Typical mid eighteenth-century, elaborate, rococo-
inspired, decorative handle, usually made of gilt.

 p. 45

George III, English c. 1760–1790
Very simple elegance of a lightly decorated ring handle to a mahogany drawer front featuring a small keyhole above.

 1760 p. 42

George III, English c. 1775–1810
Stamped back-plate and integral drop ring emphasising the circular motif of the inlays forming the contrasting timbers of a drawer front. Various designs and shapes based on this idea exist.

 1775 p. 60

George III to Regency, English c. 1790–1830
Small, finely detailed, circular drawer pull with a circular stamped back-plate. Various motifs exist in this style.

 1790 p. 60

George III to William IV, English c. 1800–1830
Neoclassicism applied to a gilt ring handle with a lion's mask motif, a variant of many such handles were designed, but here it is purely decorative.

 1800 p. 64

🎴 LEGS 🎴

THE PREOCCUPATION with Classical Antiquity runs as a
theme through the centuries of leg design and reflects changing
tastes and fashions when studied with the foot of a piece.

Egyptian, New Kingdom (18th Dynasty) c. 1330 BC

One of the earliest surviving chair legs in history from Tutankhamen's tomb. Characterised by its carved symbolic lions' masks, feet and turned support with gold leaf.

Regency, English c. 1815

Ebonised, carved beechwood leg with gilt enrichments to leopard's mask, pelt anthemion leaf and paw foot. A direct reference to contemporary archaeological discoveries. In the manner of George Smith.

Regency, English c. 1815

Stylised, carved, ebonised, beechwood lion's leg and gilt paw foot of a highly fashionable armchair. Reflects the interest aroused by Thomas Hope's designs for furniture based on Antique sources.

Regency, English c. 1820

Forceful, carved giltwood lion's paw foot of an outswept leg. The decoration is from Antique Roman foliate designs.

Queen Anne, English c. 1710
Japanned, tri-form cabriole leg terminating in a pointed toe. An English refinement of continental examples.

William and Mary, English c. 1695
The advent of the sensational new 's-scroll leg fashionably japanned. This shape derived from continental forms imported by foreign craftsmen, many following William and Mary.

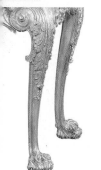

George II, English c. 1730
Elaborately carved technical feat enabling the support of a massive marble-topped table. Gilt-gesso carved leg with acanthus leaf on the knee and hairy paw foot.

1730   p. 45

George II, English c. 1740
Mahogany card-table leg carved with an acanthus leaf to the knee, claw-and-ball foot inspired by Antique Roman examples. Tensile strength of high quality timber permits the slim profile of the leg.

1740   p. 45

George II, English c. 1740
Profusely carved giltwood chair leg. Rococo
foliate patterns merge with the hairy
Antique pattern of cabriole leg and
paw foot.

     p. 45

George II, English c. 1745
Stylised, carved acanthus leaf on knee of a
rounded mahogany cabriole leg. The claw-
and-ball foot and leaf derived from
Antique Roman designs.

     p. 45

George II, English c. 1730
Carved claw paw and acanthus leaf carved mahogany knee. Imperial Roman design sources defined a cultured household.

George II, English c. 1745
Carved cabriole leg pushed to the extremity of practical form. Tough mahogany used for crisp, leafy knee carving and claw-and-ball foot .

George II, English c. 1755
Hipped, mahogany library chair cabriole
leg with flamboyant leafy carving. The
powerfully carved claw-and-ball foot was
at the height of its fashion.

1775 p. 42

Queen Anne, English c. 1710
Rounded wing-chair seat frieze supporting
subtly shaped leg. Shorter cabriole leg with
favourite shell motif.

1710 p. 40

Queen Anne, English c. 1710
Discreetly modelled early cabriole shape of a walnut chair leg with a pad foot. Subtle colour of the timber obviating all extra decoration.

     1710 p. 38

George III, English c. 1760
Highly decorative carved knee of a salon chair. Robust rococo-scrolled naturalistic toe on a disc base.

      1760 p. 50

Queen Anne, English c. 1710
Early form of a solid walnut standard cabriole shape with flat pad foot. Minimal shaped decoration enhances the golden colour of the timber.

     1710 *p. 38*

Queen Anne, English c. 1710
The epitome of carved cabriole-legged elegance in walnut; with early rococo 'c' scrolls, Baroque stylised shell within anthemion shape, and naturalistic claw-and-ball foot.

     1710 *p. 40*

George I, English c. 1715
Hipped cabriole leg with carved stylised shell motif to the knee and a claw-and-ball foot on an armchair.

George I, English c. 1715
Flowing, carved shell motif encasing the knee of a slim moulded cabriole leg on a thin pad foot all supporting a wing chair.

George II, English c. 1740
Sculptural decorative short cabriole leg
as a foot, modelled after an Antique
Roman example, the tightly carved acanthus
leaf knee above a lion's claw foot clutching
a rock.

 1740 p. 45

Queen Anne, English c. 1710
Dynamic carved claw-and-ball foot refined by
a useful caster and sparsely carved details on
the knee of a walnut wing chair.

 1710 p. 38

Queen Anne, English c. 1705
Early form of walnut cabriole leg, incorporating the earlier angled knee and carved division, merged with the new cabriole shape on a circular pad foot.

    1705 p. 38

Queen Anne, English c. 1710
Advanced cabriole leg with 's' shape and carved division. The angled shape is already rounded and pad foot more fully shaped.

      1710 p. 40

Queen Anne, English c. 1710

Sophisticated finely coloured walnut, round, cabriole leg. Subtly shaped knee and full pad foot are evident.

1710   p. 40

George I, English c. 1720

Advanced form of cabriole leg design with scrolled knee decoration emanating from boldly ribbed clasping leaf and supported by a tripartite triffid foot.

1720   p. 40

George II, English c. 1740
Hipped, carved mahogany cabriole leg for a stool with a profusion of naturalistic leaf decoration to the knee and a naturalistic lion's paw foot. Paw and knee decoration typifies William Kent's designs.

 1740 p. 40

George II, English c. 1745
Elegantly shaped mahogany chair leg supporting a drop-in seat and terminating in a claw-and-ball foot.

 1745 p. 42

George II, English c. 1745
Attenuated walnut cabriole leg of a table with shaped veneered frieze. Venetian influences visible in carved shell, sea, vegetation and unusual foliate decorated rounded pad foot.

1745   p. 38

George I, English c. 1725
Very delicately carved giltwood table cabriole leg. High quality carving of leaves and naturalistic foliate foot, a rare luxury in the manner of James Moore.

1725   p. 40

George I, English c. 1715
Robust walnut elegance with turned legs imitating the cabriole fashion supporting a marble-topped centre table. The carved lappets at the knee already outmoded.

1715 p. 38

George I, English c. 1720
Refined, slim-profiled, cabriole table leg with a carved knee and pad foot in the height of early Georgian fashion.

1720 p. 40

George II, English c. 1750
Heavy marble-topped mahogany console
table with carefully gauged shaped cabriole
leg enhanced with a bold acanthus leaf at
the knee and strong claw-and-ball foot,
parodying Antique Roman designs.

1750 **p. 42**

George III, English c. 1765
Simple flowing-shaped carved, moulded
leg of a mahogany table with scrolled
toe. The design is one popularised by
Thomas Chippendale.

1765 **p. 46**

George I, English c. 1715

Rare, early attenuated cabriole leg with refined shape and japanned decoration for centre silver or tea table with a tray top.

1715 p. 40

George III, English c. 1775

Attenuated, moulded and carved cabriole leg of close-grained mahogany, featuring tiny circular feet with leafy toes and stylised anthemion design on the knee. Highly sophisticated design influenced by Chippendale and the Linnell brothers.

1775 p. 46

George II, English c. 1740
Carved Vitruvian scrolled frieze of a walnut card table and equally bold acanthus carved, hipped knee of curvaceous cabriole leg. The powerful claw-and-ball foot allied to the design indicate the influence of William Kent.

George III, English c. 1765
Pointed pad foot of a sinuous variant of a cabriole leg, the base of a mahogany tripod table, embellished with neoclassical carving.

Tudor, English c. 1520

Straightforward oak leg as the extension of the frame of a pierced carved side table-cupboard. Rough appearance ameliorated by smoothed edges due to use and good proportions.

Jacobean, English c. 1615

Slender baluster turned leg of an oak framed armchair. A vernacular variant of continually used medieval styles popular into the nineteenth century in many areas.

Elizabethan, English c. 1600

Elegantly inverted baluster design of an oak leg for a joint stool; the robust feet and solid construction are durable and capable of adornment.

    p. 22

William and Mary, English c. 1690

Spiral or barley-twist turned walnut legs with double goblet turning beneath the frieze and extending through a flat stretcher to bun feet.

    p. 34

Charles II, English c. 1680

A complicated transitional carved beechwood leg with shaped cup over an 's' scroll baluster and a moulded, panelled section as a stretcher terminal above a square leaf-carved foot toe. Based upon Renaissance interpretations of Antique Classical designs.

    **1680** p. 28

William and Mary, English c. 1700

A lively reworking in turned walnut of the elements forming a basic joint stool: short baluster turnings and an outswept foliate 'Braganza' toe.

     **1700** p. 34

Charles II, English c. 1690

Fully attenuated baluster, turned walnut table leg, with double stretcher terminals, the lower forming part of the stretcher proper. Outswept foliate 'Braganza' toe.

   1690 p. 29

Charles II, English c. 1675
Spiral or barley twist, turned walnut chair leg with double stretcher terminals for upper front and lower supports, terminals as turned bobbins.

Queen Anne, English c. 1710
Remarkable variant of a walnut chair front leg, with slim turned upper terminal and outswept rounded slim paw foot.

George III, English
c. 1765

Conventional chamfered, square moulded mahogany from leg of a library chair emanating from an upholstered frieze and united with other legs by a slim tenoned stretcher. Fitted casters are visible.

George III, English
c. 1765

Elaborately carved cluster column mahogany front leg of a library chair. A masterpiece of technical skill in retaining strength, whilst exhibiting a mixture of neoclassical and Gothic elegance.

Victorian, English c. 1880
Simple, timeless, turned beech chair leg exhibiting
doweled structure utilising basic shapes refined little
over the centuries and found in vernacular furniture
such as Windsor chairs.

George III, English c. 1765
Devised from ancient Chinese furniture designs,
the lattice backed chair typically mixes Gothic
patterns. Square chamfered leg with curved
square section bracket.

George III, English c. 1780
Subtly carved, tapered and turned mahogany front
chair leg with neoclassical details popularised by
Adam, including acanthus and fluted shaft. Small
tapering round toe.

George III, English
c. 1785
Integral flowing line from arm to toe of simply shaped, decorated beechwood armchair. Square, tapered and slim front leg and outswept rear leg strengthened by uniting stretcher.

George III, English
c. 1775
Neoclassical taste and high fashion implicit in ultra-slim turned and fluted beechwood front leg decorated in off-white and gilt. The sophisticated shape of the rear leg is the mark of a master craftsman.

George III, English
c. 1790

Slim turned and tapered, ebonised beechwood front chair leg fitted into a curved shaped frieze with a tenoned block top and slim tapering toe with delicate gilt trompe l'oeil decoration.

George III, English
c. 1800

Elegantly turned, tapering, beechwood front chair leg with rounded panelled corner motif above gilt-ring decoration of the shaft and tapering kick-out toe.

George III, English c. 1780
Sophisticated, turned, fluted and tapering beechwood front chair leg with swollen 'melon' outline beneath elaborate frieze and lower arm sections. Derived from French neoclassical examples.

p. 50

George III, English c. 1795
Exuberantly detailed, turned mahogany sofa front leg with a playful neoclassical turned twist, beneath a striking lower arm terminal moulded into the leg. Attenuated toe and caster.

p. 42

George III, English c. 1780

Giltwood, turned, tapered, carved and fluted front chair leg in the neoclassical taste inspired by French Louis XVI examples.

George III, English c. 1780

Attenuated, turned, carved and stop-fluted neoclassical mahogany table leg with tapering toe; the overall length achieved by using very close-grained timber of high tensile strength.

Victorian, English c. 1895
Simple elegance in an oak chair with
slim components, most notably the legs
with minimal decoration.

George V, English c. 1925
Basic turned and dowelled members forming a strong timeless shape utilised for vernacular furniture such as the Windsor chair.

Elizabeth II, English c. 1955
The traditional turned beechwood construction of vernacular furniture given an updated fashionable twist reflecting the spiky legs of the 1950s. Characterised by strong shapes with curves and angular planes blended.

Regency, English c. 1815
An opulent form of neoclassicism utilising fine mahogany in a bergère chair front leg embellished with lustrous ormolu mounts and fitted with a bold caster.

Regency, English c. 1820
Melon-shaped, neoclassical-inspired, short, gilt-embellished, carved foot of an imposing Canterbury with gilded toe.

George III, English
c. 1790
Standard square tapered leg of a mahogany card table with decorative stringing applied to the corners, a subtle embellishment peculiarly English in execution.

George III, English c. 1790
Satinwood, square tapering table leg with very fine stringing to the corners and decorative inlays delineating the shelf. Slim spade toes suggest added refinement.

George III, English c. 1775
Moulded, square tapering leg with a stepped spade toe of extreme elegance. Colour, patina and figure of the wood are all perfect.

  p. 54

Regency, English c. 1825
Slightly bulbous, turned, fluted, mahogany and rosewood leg with a 'melon' outline fitted to a dumb waiter or buffet. Design related to both tiers. Brass toes and imposing casters.

   p. 62

Victorian, English c. 1850
*A Renaissance revival: slim, square
tapering fruitwood leg with acanthus
capital and moulded panel.*

Victorian, English c. 1880
*Intricately carved turned leg with
'Oriental' decoration based on
Middle Eastern design catering for
High Victorian exoticism.*

Victorian, English c. 1855
Lacquered, carved cabriole leg of Louis XV; revival pattern typical of Victorian taste for mixing styles and influences with slight regard for historical accuracy.

Victorian, English c. 1845
Pierced fret 'c' outline for the feet of an ebonised and gilt octagonal table with Gothic touches.

George VI, English
c. 1950
Ingeniously elegant use of
laminated bentwood, combined
arm and leg component for a
light open armchair.

George VI, English
c. 1950
Inventive use of
steamed and laminated
bentwood on folding
armchair leg supports.

George VI, English c. 1948
*Double end supports for a drop-leaf table
with uniting plinth and stepped shaped
feet: an updating of medieval English
vernacular forms.*

Elizabeth II, English
c. 1960
*The fashionably turned and tapering
stiletto leg of a coffee table in its heyday.
Structurally unsound at the joint, even
with stretchers.*

Regency, English c. 1810
Ebonised early nineteenth-century 'x'-frame leg of supreme elegance of line copying Antique examples. Tending to break across the grain; expensive high fashion.

p. 62

Victorian, English c. 1865
An essay in medievalist historicism akin to Renaissance 'x'-framed chairs, but over-indulgent with superfluous supports.

p. 74

Regency, English c. 1810

Painted and gilt beechwood neoclassical front chair leg, termed a sabre leg in reference to the Napoleonic Wars of the time. Tend to break across the grain if of inferior timber.

Regency, English c. 1810

Neoclassical, decorated, and beechwood day-bed foot based on Ancient neoclassical designs and patterned with simulated ormolu mounts. Typical caster.

MIRRORS

AMONGST THE most fragile items of furniture and reliant
upon advances in glass manufacture, mirrors are a barometer
of changing fashions in carved furniture styles, and were
clearly the commissions of rich patrons.

**Charles II, English
c. 1685**
*A remarkable survival of
an early large framed
mirror. The early cushion
frame of convex moulding
is here pierce fretted and
given profuse carved
decoration. Note also the
retention of the shaped
cornice, here with a coronet
and the cypher of the
original owner.*

George I, English c. 1725
Expensive sheets of glass were even more valuable when mirrored. A tiny piece gives a purely decorative patch of light to the interior of a bureau when placed on a small door.

   p. 36

George I, English c. 1725
Large plates of mirrored and bevelled glass enhance the upper doors of a bureau bookcase; the bevels follow the line of the frame.

     p. 36

George I, English
c. 1715
Gilt furniture often
encompassed matching
mirrors. Delicate carved
frame enhanced by
intricate detail carved in
wood and gesso, the
architectural cornice a
work of art reflecting the
interior design and often
a matching side-table.

**George I, English
c. 1715**
*Practical mirror frame
embellishing the carved
giltwood frame with
a pair of candle-arms:
the reflected light
magnified for a dull
evening and enhancing
the mirror frame.*

George II, English c. 1735
The influence of William
Kent's designs typified by the
strong architectural outline of
the frame; the shell motifs,
favourite devices on a grand
scale with a large plate.

George II, English c. 1745

Neo-Palladian influence visible in the outline of this carved gilt and gesso frame overlaid with intricate rocaille decoration, a peculiarly English style of supreme elegance, incorporating a large and valuable piece of glass.

George III, English c. 1760
Full-blown English rococo of carved gilt pine with a frame of varied 'c' scrolls and rocaille detail surmounted by a perching bird; the frame apparently subdividing the glass. In the style of Chippendale.

George III, English c. 1760

Carved gilt pine girandoles – mirrors as decorative lighting fixtures with candle arms and in the full rococo manner – fashionable in the middle years of the eighteenth century.

George II, English c. 1750

Controlled form of English giltpine carving surrounding a design of two mirror plates within sprays of naturalistic flowers and leaves.

George III, English c. 1765
Sculptural girandole with formally
arranged, deeply carved pine replicating
scrolled acanthus leaves; the definite heart
shape a motif often used by Robert Adam.

George III, English c. 1760
Huge mirror forming part of a
decorative scheme. Rectangular plate
subdivided by trailing foliate giltwood
fillets, and bold outline has carved gilt
pine garlands surmounted by a large
neoclassical urn.

George III, English c. 1770
Highly refined design for a giltwood frame with decorative patterns and surmounted by an Adamesque final urn and trailing foliage.

p. 54

Regency, English c. 1810
Central section of a giltwood and gesso decorated overmantel incorporating a convex mirror, an early example of a favourite Regency device.

p. 62

Regency, English c. 1815
Giltwood convex mirror wit[h]
lavishly decorated frame
incorporating candle arms a[nd]
symbols of war: victor's leave[s]
musket balls and stars – all
typical motifs used on furnit[ure]
of the period.

Regency, English c. 1815
Naval battles and victories of
the Napoleonic Wars clearly
a topic of fashionable
decoration as demonstrated
by the inclusion of rope
motifs, stars and musket balls.

George V, English c. 1928
*Arched mirror framed by open metalwork in a
style derived from pre-First World War Austro-
German decoration, later refined by the French
during the 1920s and now known as Art Deco.*

George V, English
c. 1910
Unusual use of a mirror frame in the hands of a sculptor; the giltwood frame with an incised chevron motif and romantic inscription.

William and Mary,
English c. 1690
Cushion-framed mirror with a kingwood frame, embellished with panels of floral marquetry derived from Dutch examples.

GETTING STARTED

Introduction

THIS book indicates the basic knowledge necessary for the person seeking information on the many aspects of furniture appreciation. Identification of the age and styles of a piece is the first step in attempting to clarify a range of requirements, such as quality of design, construction, materials used and conception of the overall design.

It is impossible to have any idea of any of these categories without experience of a wide variety of objects. Careful study of a particular category, say chairs of a certain date and style, is vital if you are looking for a particular piece. This book will help you to identify a piece of furniture by examining such features as legs. It is up to you to then make your field of research as wide as possible.

Collections of furniture in local museums and national ones, such as the Victoria and Albert Museum in London, will display useful examples of furniture of all periods and styles. Similar furniture may also be seen in the many houses open to the public. Dealers and auctioneers will also have an interesting selection of items and, with permission, you will be able to handle the items on view and use your own eyes.

This book tells you how to begin looking at British furniture. You should read the history and stylistic detail sections with particular attention and bear in mind that specialising in your favourite area will enable you to appreciate the complexities and possibilities that a study of British furniture will afford you.

An antique dealer's showroom, with a variety of furniture.

Buying and Selling

WHATEVER you buy should be acquired because you truly love it, whether inexpensive or expensive. Whatever you acquire has to fit comfortably into your home and be sympathetic to its surroundings and you. The bargain you thought you were getting may necessitate an expensive new decorative scheme, so think very carefully about the utility of what you are buying.

Many people believe that in buying an antique or old piece

of furniture they are instantly gaining an investment; in the short-term this is seldom the case even if the piece is the best of its type or you have an extraordinary eye and luck. Competition is now so keen that prices are high even for rubbish. It is best to examine as many examples of a piece as possible and decide on your own price level. The best examples of furniture do tend to hold their value and increase with time, but it may be decades before you see your 'investment' pay off.

ANTIQUE DEALERS

IT SEEMS OBVIOUS, but the best pieces are generally found in the stock of reputable dealers belonging to the main organisations, such as the British Antique Dealers Association (BADA), who will guarantee authenticity. A good dealer will discuss his stock and answer your questions about restoration.

The major auction houses also provide a range of goods and services and you can take your chance and bid for pieces, if you are really satisfied about their authenticity. You should also visit the many antique fairs to assess the market for buying and selling and train your own eyes as far as possible if you wish to enjoy the experience.

Ebonised and gilt beechwood chairs, with leopard's head and anthemion design inspired by Antique Greek examples revived by Thomas Hope et al.

Where to Buy

JUST as you would not seek out a car mechanic to work on your teeth, so you should not be persuaded to part with large sums of money for a piece unless convinced of its authenticity. When doubtful, buy from an established dealer belonging to any of the following:

The British Antique Dealers Association (BADA)

The London and Provincial Arts and Antique Dealers Association (LAPADA)

Confederation International des Negociants en Objets d'Art (CINOA)

There is also a wide variety of auction rooms nationally, most of which have elaborate clauses relating to their responsibilities to the purchaser. If in any doubt, check objects and your rights before you purchase. Afterwards may not be too late, but can be time-consuming and upsetting in the event of mistakes.

Your own eyes and knowledge will be endlessly tantalised, rewarded and expanded by ever-changing items to be seen. Learning is the greatest fun, but there is no substitute for a 'hands-on' approach. Be very wary of buying stolen goods at markets or boot fairs. Even the vendor may not be fully aware of the source of the goods.

Simple but attenuated square tapering oak back framework, with shaped horizontal backsplats embracing a pierced fretwork heart motif – a particularly favourite device of C. A. Voysey, c. 1895.

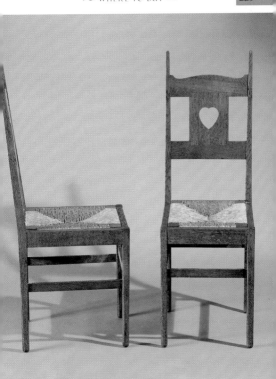

Auctions and Antique Shops

ASSUME that having absorbed the information in this book you will wish to spend some of your hard-earned cash on a piece of British furniture. Where do you go? The first rule is that you should define your field and price range.

There are some excellent guides to antique shops in Britain. Look at entries for your locality and see what their speciality is. If you enjoy looking, visit them all, fairs included. Otherwise you can telephone and ask if they have what you are looking for. Many shops now have door-bells so just ring: most dealers are overjoyed to see a polite customer showing enthusiastic interest, whether you buy or not. No matter how grand or small the shop or fair-stand, always ask before you touch anything.

SELLING YOUR ANTIQUES

IF YOU ARE CONSIDERING selling a piece, look at several examples and then consider the price range. You will find a visit to the local auction room useful, for the price of an object is determined by how much a person will pay. It is not the dealers who pay the inflated prices and they will also buy privately. Usually sale-room fever affects peoples' egos and bids soar – therefore a sample price may be unrealistically high. This can be an advantage to you as the seller, but try to be realistic. An auctioneer will want your business and his estimate is only a rough guide. In a shop, a dealer has to include overheads into the buying and selling price, but may pay you a fair price

Walnut and upholstery Queen Anne stool.

immediately. You should inform yourself beforehand of the value of your piece and set your own price accordingly, with a little flexibility, just as you would if selling your house. Blindly asking for offers from a position of complete ignorance is asking for dissatisfaction.

Where to View

A PART from dealers' premises and auction houses, there is a wealth of useful information to be gleaned by examining the contents of houses open to the public. Amongst the best are those still lived in and loved by the heirs of those who built them and collected the many objects within.

There are various excellent guidebooks concerning opening hours and contents; an excursion can prove more rewarding than an hour in a sale-room, even if most of the items on view are now virtually impossible to buy.

Instructive television programmes, such as the *Antiques Roadshow* are also useful. Museums exist in major and minor locations. London is fortunate in possessing the Victoria and Albert Museum and a string of houses with important pieces on view. Smaller museums, such as Preston Manor in Brighton, are no less important in displaying minor pieces of great historical importance and of interest to the furniture enthusiast trying to understand the many levels of furniture production and design, when set against a unique series of interiors, such as those in Brighton Pavilion. Again, a good guide will indicate these and the many properties now in the hands of the National Trust, including some recent additions from the 1930s.

In addition to viewing furniture, connoisseurs will also familiarise themselves with the objects in use during their favoured period. Collections of porcelain or silver are subjects in their own right, but were not conceived in a vacuum. The clothing of the period visible in paintings or on dummies in museums is also an adjunct to furniture design and often explains the exaggerated shape of, for example, some types of chair.

Carved and inlaid oak armchair in the Victoria and Albert Museum.

UNDERSTANDING FURNITURE
Introduction

> The aesthetic appeal and utility of a piece of furniture are undoubtedly vital to any owner and prospective puchaser. However, it is also true that beauty is skin-deep. How do you know that the piece in front of you is what you think or hope it is ?

IN the age of any piece we look at the style. Remember: styles have notoriously been faked at worst, or copied at best. If you have done your homework, then you will have an initial inkling from the price tag that a piece is not what it should be and the vendor may have made a mistake. In short, a sound technical knowledge is necessary, as are a pair of very keen eyes and some common sense.

RECOGNISING MODIFICATIONS

YOU WILL HAVE to acquaint yourself with many examples of a piece, study the timbers used and the construction or interior, as applicable. Replacements of feet and handles may be irrelevant in a good piece, but may ruin an indifferent one. What was part of a fashionable updating can be undone, but a botched change can ruin a piece.

Furniture represents our own changing civilisation. You should not be indifferent to the history of furniture, for this knowledge will inform you of so much about the use of timbers, and enable you to put components in their correct context. You may use a piece quite differently from its original function, but it pays to know what that function was in order to appreciate quality of design and construction.

Regency, c. 1815, giltwood convex mirror incorporating candle arms and symbols of war including victor's leaves, musket balls and stars.

Types of Wood

THE history of furniture is noted for periodic use of different woods. The main dates and woods are as follows:

- Oak (*Quercus*), from earliest times until today, but predominently from 1500–1650. Again in Victorian times.
- Walnut (*Juglans*), from about 1640–1740. Again in Victorian times.
- Pine (*Pinus*), deal (Norwegian or Baltic pine) and fir, from 1640.
- Elm (*Ulmus*), early and country furniture, from 1500.
- Yewood (*Taxus*), early and country furniture, from 1500.
- Beech (*Fagus*), from 1660 and for country furniture.
- Ash (*Frorcinus*), country furniture and Victorian cabinet-making.

IMPORTED TIMBERS

- Deal (see above).
- Mahogany (*Swietenia*), known in England by 1680, predominantly after 1730 (West Indies, Cuba, South America).
- Satinwood (*Chloroxylon swietenia*), from about 1760, (West Indies, India, South America).
- Tulipwood (*Liriodendron tulipifera*) for bandings (North American).
- Rosewood (various types).
- Ebony (*Diospyros*) Ceylon.
- Calamander (*Diospyrus*) India.
- Maple (*Acer*) Canada. Victorian, from Victorian times.

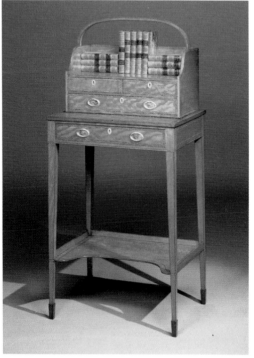

Satinwood cheveret dating from the reign of George III, c. 1790.

Techniques

IN reading the sections of this book it will be apparent that the development of furniture styles is heavily dependent upon the technology available to the craftsman.

The use of mortice and tenon joints was only general by the late 1400s. Until the 1700s there is no doubt that Britain lagged behind the rest of Europe in design and skills and that it was the immigration of skilled craftsmen which so radically altered this. The use of chisels, adze, and saw-pits was usual.

The styles of the sixteenth century are stolid copies of much that had happened in the cities of Holland and Germany, but only with rising prosperity and a new monarch, Charles II, used to sophisticated French taste from his exile, did British taste develop and demand new novelties, such as dovetail joints on drawers.

SEVENTEENTH-CENTURY REVOLUTION

MORE SKILLED TURNING of wood, the introduction of the plane and the use of lighter construction are all part of the revolution in taste that occurred after 1660. The Dutch monarch William of Orange was also the catalyst for a whole new school of thought, introducing veneer and marquetry craftsmen into England. These workers laid the ground for the carvers and cabinet-makers of the remarkable years of the eighteenth century.

The introduction of some cutting machinery by the 1790s ensured that an assembly line approach to furniture-making was introduced, but quality was rapidly sacrificed for quantity during the nineteenth century. Thin-cut veneers and the use of plywood were usual in mid-Victorian England, with steam presses forming yards of furniture components covered with wafer-thin veneers for mass markets all over the world. The hand-made piece of furniture only became appreciated again after about 1870 with the advent of the Arts and Crafts movement. Yet even machine-made furniture can have a charm and is worthy of our attention.

Arts and Crafts-influenced hand-made chair by Charles Rennie Mackintosh.

Care of Furniture

All furniture should be treated with care and respect. If you look after it well, it should give you service and pleasure for ever.

 A PART from dusting, regular waxing with a good colourless furniture wax is essential. It is better to use wax in small quantities with a good soft duster and not let it dry. This not only gives a beautiful sheen to the surfaces, but also nourishes and moisturises the wood. Avoid spray-on polishes, as they can leave patchy finishes and build up odd residues and surfaces. Similarly, buffing up brass handles can leave white encrustations on the surrounding timber. Be extra careful!

Veneered furniture is particularly susceptible to climatic variations and can easily shed sections of veneer. This is why a humidifier is a good idea in controlled situations, but not if it simply makes changes of humidity even more variable when doors or windows are opened and shut. A bowl of water in which a sponge forms a reservoir is by far the best solution for a cabinet piece or one with drawers. Place the bowl in the lowest drawer and the carcase of the piece will naturally absorb or reject the moisture available. Avoid draughts on all wooden furniture.

RESTORATION

IF SOMETHING IS chipped or scratched, or if veneers are shed, do not panic. Keep any loose pieces carefully. Always obtain the very best professional advice. If unsure, speak to a reputable dealer with a stock of furniture looking the way you would like your damaged piece to be. Obtain more than one estimate and remember that by choosing a cheap and cheerful solution you can inflict terrible damage to your treasured possession. Do not stint on careful maintenance, any more than you would with a mechanical possession such as your car.

Oak swan chair by C. F. Voysey, c. 1898.

Valuing and Insuring

Y OU should immediately insure your new possession for the price you have paid and naturally keep any invoices or receipts as proof, together with photographs. Many people now mark their possessions with invisible marker pens in case of theft.

Owning any possessions is perhaps stressful, so consider installing or overhauling your alarm system and security. Both

your local police and insurer will give advice on measures to be taken. Fine art insurers also exist, they are not necessarily more expensive and are often more understanding of your problems.

GETTING YOUR ANTIQUES VALUED

OBTAINING updated valuations is usually done by asking the vendor to supply you with one from time to time. Most dealers will not charge for this, if the piece originally formed part of their stock. You should always enquire first if there is a charge involved and have this explained to you. Some reputable dealers will also value your possessions and you should look for one with experience in your type of collection.

Auction houses also give valuations and may well be the best solution for you if you need a complete house valuation. This can then be added to, and updated, from time to time.

Specialist valuers exist for special collections and will provide a scale of fees, normally depending on the time involved in examining your possessions. These are not normally used for general valuations.

Insurance and valuations are regrettably necessary and expensive adjuncts to owning pleasing pieces, but they will provide peace of mind.

Ebonised beechwood chairs with slim turned and tapered legs, dating from c. 1790.

COMPENDIUM
Glossary

Acanthus leaf: The leaf of a herbaceaous plant used in Antique architecture as an adornment for Corinthian and Composite capital and extensively used in stylised forms after 1660 on carved English furniture. Rarely used after *c.* 1914.

Adze: An axe-like implement, but with the blade curving towards the handle like a solid hoe; used for reducing the surface of timber and even smoothing it.

Arcading: A form of carved decoration utilising a series of arches on raised pilasters set against a solid ground timber.

Art Deco: A term derived from the 1925 *Paris Exposition des arts décoratifs*. First used by museum curators in Paris in the late 1950s to describe the style current at the exhibition and just after.

Art Moderne: Descriptive term for the decorative applied arts following Art Deco (q.v.) and exhibiting streamlined curvaceaous lines.

Art Nouveau: The sinuous plant-like outlines and applied decorations popular in France during the 1890s and early 1900s; known in Italy as 'Stile Liberty' and Germany and Austria 'Jugendstil'.

Arts and Crafts movement: Developed by William Morris and other adherents of anti-mass production; developed as an aesthetic based on pre-industrial craftsmanship and updated solid 'medieval' designs of native timbers. The movement used minimal decorative devices.

Astragal mouldings: A small, semi-circular moulded section of wood.

Back-plate: The retaining metal fitting of a handle fixed to the wooden front of a drawer.

Backsplat: An upright section of wood, frequently carved, infilling the framework of the back of a chair or settee.

Bakelite: Artificial resin invented in 1913 by L. H. Baekeland and very popular in use as a plastic.

Baluster (leg): Short pillar, bulging below and narrow above, based on the blossom of the wild pomegranate.

Barley twist: Turning of an upward and downward spiral, named after barley sugar sticks.

Baroque: A florid form of neo-classicism used in late-Renaissance Europe and then in Britain.

Bent-plywood: Sheets of thin timber glued together under pressure and shaped by a steam-press process.

Bentwood: Modern components shaped by a steaming press process.

Bergère: A form of upholstered armchair of generous proportions, derived from French examples.

Bobbin turnings: Turnings achieved on a wooden spindle, in the shape of a bobbin.

Boulle-work: Brass inlays in flat patterns imitating the work of Charles André Boulle (French, late-seventeenth century).

Bracket feet: Flat block-shaped feet given a scrolled

outline in the form of a bracket.

Bun feet: Feet of a piece in the shape of a compressed spherical bun.

Buttoned: Upholstery held tightly by strategically placed buttons covered in fabric.

Cabriole leg: A sinuous 'S'-shaped leg emanating from the Continent and fashionable in England *c.* 1700–60.

Camel-backed (settee): An undulating, humped top-rail of the back.

Canted corner: A bevelled corner.

Case furniture: Usually meaning anything with a box-like structure.

Chamfered: An edge bevelled off from the piece.

Chinoiserie: A form of decoration imitating Far Eastern, usually Chinese, motifs.

Claw-and-ball foot: A foot carved to resemble a lion's paw or eagle's claws around a ball.

Cleated: A butterfly-shaped piece of wood inset with a flat surface across a closed crack or split to prevent it opening again.

Cornice: A horizontal moulded projecting piece usually decorated at the top of a cabinet.

Cotswold School: A loose description of craftsmen working in the region in the Arts and Crafts tradition.

Crocket: Ornamental Gothic device of buds or curled leaves on the sides of pinnacles.

Dentil cornice: Small rectangular blocks regularly

spaced under the base moulding of a cornice.

Dovetail joint: A tenon cut in the shape of a dove's tail, made to fit into a mortice (q.v.) of corresponding shape – and vice versa.

Drop-in seat: A seat frame made and upholstered separately from a chair and held in a moulded frame-work.

Drop-leaf table: A table with a flat top concealing in its double thickness a with-drawable leaf at each end, the top falling into the vacant space when these are extended.

Fiddle-back figuring: Term pplied to the highly curled figures of mahogany used on violin cases.

Finial: A turned piece of decorative wood, often urn- or vase-shaped, placed on top of a cabinet.

Flame figuring: Figure or pattern of the grain, usually in mahogany, resembling a flame.

Fluted cluster-column legs: Legs formed in the design of a group or 'cluster' of slender columns with incised concave vertical indentations or 'flutes'.

Formica: Extremely tough form of heat resistant plastic sheeting, with various colours and patterns applied by gluing to flat surfaces of tables.

Franco-Italian Renaissance style: The fashionable forms of neoclassicism evolved from Italian and French styles used in the Renaissance.

Fretted carving: Linear cut decoration of intersecting thin pieces of wood of trellis patterns.

Frieze: Architectural term also applied to furniture; the decorative piece between architrave (moulded frame of e.g. a door) and cornice.

Galleries: Ornamental borders to a top in the form of small parapets or railings.

Gate-leg: A form of hinged table support resembling a gate under a raised flap.

Gesso: A paste made of a ground plaster compound and glue applied to timber surfaces and smoothed for decorative effects or gilding.

Gothic: Architectural and decorative style notable for pointed arches derived from Islamic patterns and popular in Europe *c.* 1100–1500. Revived seriously in the nineteenth century and as fantasy in the eighteenth century as 'Gothick'.

Hairy paw feet: Feet carved as hairy animal paws.

Half bobbins: Turned decoration resembling half a bobbin.

Half-tester: Canopy of a bed usually fixed to a wall over the head, extending only halfway.

Hutch: A storage chest, coffer or cupboard, usually with pierced decoration as ventilation.

Inlay: The insertion of one shaped piece of wood veneer or metal into the cut-out prepared surface of another for decorative purposes.

Japanning: A form of painted flat decoration imitating Chinese lacquer.

Japonais: Decorative designs imitating Far Eastern and Japanese patterns.

Jazz-modern: A term given to spurious 'modernistic' fragmented angular decoration, usually employing a zig-zag motif.

Joint stool: A stool of solid timber joined by willow pegs or dowels driven through the joints.

Kick-out toe: The toe of a chair turning out at an angle of 45 degrees.

Klismos chair: A chair design imitating Antique Greek examples with wide scooped top-rails and outswept square tapering legs.

Knoll chair: The firm of Knoll pioneered the use of simple forms utilising applied industrial technology.

Lacquer: A resinous varnish taking a hard polish and applied in many layers, each one dried and rubbed down before the next is put on top.

Linenfold: A carved or moulded attenuated panel ornament resembling a fold of linen.

Loo table: Victorian occasional table originally used for the card game Loo.

Low boy: A small early eighteenth century four-legged low side-table with a deep frieze containing an arrangement of drawers.

Marquetry: A form of intricately patterned inlay utilising various shapes and colours of wood veneer, usually of floral design.

Modernistic: Decorative pattern or stark geometric outline representing a debased form of design derived from Bauhaus, New American or continental designs from the inter-war period.

Mortice and tenon joints: The insertion of a shaped end of a timber into the corresponding slot of another member to form a rigid joint.

Neoclassical: The updated versions of the Classical orders utilised in design through successive centuries.

Neo-Gothic: The updated versions of Gothic motifs utilised through successive centuries.

Ormolu: Ground gold preparation used in bronze mounts for furniture.

Pad foot: Disc moulded carved foot of a cabriole leg.

Palladian: Style of architecture and design elements derived from the works of Andrea Palladio (1518–80).

Paterae: Flat, dish-shaped ornaments in bas-relief.

Pediment: A triangular-shaped gable-like decorative device used in buildings and often as the top of cabinets.

Pegged joints: Joints held by pegs driven through drilled holes.

Pembroke table: A small occasional table with drop leaves, supposedly named after the Countess of Pembroke who first ordered one.

Phenolite: A form of plastic derived from hydrocarbons.

Pier table: A table placed in the short wall, or pier, between two windows.

Pierced fret: Fret decoration cut out to leave a lattice-work design.

Pilaster: Square or rectangular flattened column or pillar.

Punched ground: Decoration applied to gesso, applied as small circular indentations with a tool.

Quartered-veneer: A top veneered with four pieces of timber cut from the same block and arranged to give a radiating pattern from the centre.

Rococo: A form of elaborate decoration depending on sinuous shapes embodying shells, rocks, foliate motifs and 'C' or 'S' scrolls. Popular in Europe during the early eighteenth century.

S-scroll legs: Legs formed as a scroll imitating an attenuated 'S' shape.

Sabre leg: A tapered square-shaped outswept leg derived from the Klismos chair; renamed during the period of Napoleonic wars.

Saw-pit: The hole in the ground over which tree trunks or branches were placed for the operation of large, two-man saws.

Scrolled toe: The toe of a leg ending in a pronounced scroll carving.

Shield backs: Chair backs shaped as shields popular in the late eighteenth century.

Side chair: A chair without arms.

Slab supports: Pieces of supporting timber of rectangular blockish shapes.

Small bobbins: Turned bobbin decoration of small scale.

Spindles: Turned slim decorations resembling the spindles of a spinning wheel.

Spiral turnings: Pieces of wood turned on a lathe and given a spiral twist form.

Splat: The internal back supports of a chair set within the outer framework.

Split-caned seat: A seat made of woven slit cane set in a decorative pattern.

Spoon-back: The shape of a Victorian chair back resembling the shape of a tea-caddy spoon.

Squab: A flat stuffed cushion forming the pad on a chair seat.

Staple-hinges: Hinges formed of thick iron on metal loops.

Strapwork: Attenuated linear interlocking strap-like decoration found in plaster or gesso work in the eighteenth century.

Stretcher: Interlocking base supports of horizontal form between legs.

Stuff-over: Upholstery that is carried over the framework and secured at the bottom edge or underneath.

Stump work: Raised embroidered decoration popular in the seventeenth century.

Sussex chair: Country chair of local Sussex origin formed of turned wooden members with a plaited-rush seat; revived by William Morris.

Swan's-necks: A curving design generally used for broken pediments and handle shapes.

Top-rail: The uppermost rail or top member forming a chair back.

Torchères: Derived from the French word for a stand supporting a candelabrum or lighting device.

Tripod table: A table with a columnar base supported by three legs.

Turned toe: A toe formed from a turning on a lathe with a rounded outline.

Under-scrolled toe: The reverse of a scrolled toe, whereby the carving turns back on itself.

Uprights: The vertical members constituting a frame, eg of a chair back.

Utility: A government-imposed set of standards for wartime production, specifying maximum quantities of material, labour and price allowed for specified furniture designs; recognisable by the stamped Utility 'kite' mark.

Veneer: A thin sheet of timber selected for colour, figure and often rarity to be glued on to a less attractive and possibly more durable ground timber forming the carcase of a piece of furniture.

Wedged joints: Early joints formed by inserting the tenon of a member through a mortice and securing it by driving in a wedge. Unstable and unsatisfactory. Superseded by the mortice and tenon joint held by pegs.

Windsor chairs: Like the Sussex variety, a local type of chair with turned members, but with a solid shaped seat and arms. Now used as a generic term for all such chairs of beech, yew or other wood.

Wing chair: A chair with protruding, ear-like shaped sides at the top, or 'wings' to keep off draughts.

X-framed folding chair: An early form of portable chair with a hinged x-frame, much revived over the centuries, latterly as a solid non-folding piece of furniture.

Useful Addresses and Numbers

AUCTION HOUSES

Bonhams
Montpelier Street
London SW7
Tel: 0171 393 3900

Christie's
8 King Street
St James's
London SW1
Tel: 0171 839 9060

Sotheby's
34-35 New Bond Street
London W1
Tel: 0171 493 8080

ASSOCIATIONS

Antique Collectors' Club
5 Church Street
Woodbrige
Suffolk IP12 1DS
Tel: 01394 385501

**London and Provincial
Antique Dealers' Association
(LAPADA)**
Suite 214
535 Kings Road
London SW10 0SZ
Tel: 0171 823 3511

**British Antique Dealers'
Association (BADA)**
20 Rutland Gate
London SW7 1BD
Tel: 0171 589 4128

Bibliography

Antique Furniture, John Andrews (Antique Collector's Club)

Antique Furniture Almanac, Ronal Peasall (Moffat Lochar)

Pictorial Dictionary of British 19th Century Furniture Design (Antique Collector's Club)

Regency Furniture, Frances Collard (Antique Collectors' Club)

The Dictionary of English Furniture, Ralph Edwards (Antique Collector's Club)

The Handbook of Antique Furniture, Plantagenet Somerset Fry (Barrie & Jenkins)

The National Trust Pocket Guide to Furniture, Michael Pick (Octopus)

Index

COLLINS GEM
BABIES' names
a ? z
a mine of information

COLLINS GEM
BEER
a mine of information

COLLINS GEM
BIRDS
a mine of information

COLLINS GEM
CALORIE
Counter
a mine of information

COLLINS GEM
FACT FILE
a mine of information

COLLINS GEM
FENG SHUI
a mine of information

COLLINS GEM
FLAGS
a mine of information

COLLINS GEM
Healthy EATING
a mine of information

COLLINS GEM
QUOTATIONS
a mine of information

COLLINS GEM
SAS
Self-Defence
a mine of information

COLLINS GEM
SAS
Survival Guide
a mine of information

COLLINS GEM
SEASHORE
a mine of information

COLLINS GEM
TREES
a mine of information

COLLINS GEM
Understanding DREAMS
a mine of information

COLLINS GEM
WILD flowers
a mine of information

COLLINS GEM
WINE
Dictionary
a mine of information